# THE GEORGIAN GIRL

MEMOIRS OF MARIE ZOURABOFF

*To Jen*
*With best wishes*
*Nicholas Moffitt*

Order this book online at www.trafford.com/07-1039
or email orders@trafford.com

Most Trafford titles are also available at major online book retailers.

© Copyright 2008 Nicholas McIlwraith.

All rights reserved. No part of this publication may be reproduced, stored in a retrieval system, or transmitted, in any form or by any means, electronic, mechanical, photocopying, recording, or otherwise, without the written prior permission of the author.

Note for Librarians: A cataloguing record for this book is available from Library and Archives Canada at www.collectionscanada.ca/amicus/index-e.html

Printed in Victoria, BC, Canada.

ISBN: 978-1-4251-2935-4

*We at Trafford believe that it is the responsibility of us all, as both individuals and corporations, to make choices that are environmentally and socially sound. You, in turn, are supporting this responsible conduct each time you purchase a Trafford book, or make use of our publishing services. To find out how you are helping, please visit www.trafford.com/responsiblepublishing.html*

*Our mission is to efficiently provide the world's finest, most comprehensive book publishing service, enabling every author to experience success. To find out how to publish your book, your way, and have it available worldwide, visit us online at www.trafford.com/10510*

**Trafford** PUBLISHING   www.trafford.com

**North America & international**
toll-free: 1 888 232 4444 (USA & Canada)
phone: 250 383 6864 ♦ fax: 250 383 6804 ♦ email: info@trafford.com

**The United Kingdom & Europe**
phone: +44 (0)1865 487 395 ♦ local rate: 0845 230 9601
facsimile: +44 (0)1865 481 507 ♦ email: info.uk@trafford.com

10  9  8  7  6  5  4

# THE AUTHOR

Nicholas McIlwraith is the son of Marie Zouraboff and Ian McIlwraith. He has taken the notes of his mother and, with what she has related over the years, blended them into a book, writing it in his mother's words, as he believes she would have spoken them.

# DEDICATION

These memoirs are dedicated to my children and future generations.

# LIST OF ILLUSTRATIONS

Marie Zouraboff in London circa 1930 ................................................... Front cover
Author viewing Tiflis from the Citadel ................................................... Back cover
Tsar Nicholas II greeting the French President Monsieur Poincaré ..................... 8
The Green Cape, the Zouraboff's summer house on the Black Sea ....................... 8
Marie Zouraboff aged about three ............................................................ 9
Madame Zouraboff with Lily & Marie ........................................................ 9
Madame Zouraboff – Marie's mother circa 1904 ............................................ 9
General Nicholas Zouraboff – Marie's father ............................................... 10
General Zouraboff leaving coach number 6 ................................................. 18
General Zouraboff in full military uniform ................................................ 19
Madame Zouraboff - circa 1910 ................................................................ 20
Marie in Irkutsk aged about fifteen .......................................................... 21
Marie on Chita – circa 1916 .................................................................... 22
Vladivostok sketched by Captain Savory .................................................... 34
Marie Zouraboff aged about 18 ............................................................... 38
Reginald Savory in Vladivostok ............................................................... 38
Claret Jug given to Captain Savory in Vladivostok ...................................... 38
House in Montclair, New Jersey rented by Arthur Hodges .............................. 46
Turweston House 1925 .......................................................................... 51
Marie in grounds of Turweston House ...................................................... 51
Presentation at Buckingham Palace .......................................................... 52
Marie aged 26 in Paris .......................................................................... 53
Ian McIlwraith in the car in which he & Marie drove to Devon ....................... 53
Marie with Nicky in London 1931 ............................................................ 54
Vice Admiral Alan Scott-Moncrieff on duty during WW2 ............................... 60
General Sir Reginald Savory 1969 ............................................................ 84
Sir Reginald Savory at work at School Hill Cottage ..................................... 87
Sir Reginald & Lady Savory off to a reception ............................................ 88

# PREFACE

My mother was born and spent her early years in Tiflis in Georgia. At that time and since 1800, Georgia had been a province of Tsarist Russia and Tiflis was the Russian name given to the capital city. It has now, with independence from Russia and the former Soviet Union, reverted to its name of Tbilisi. The name Tiflis is retained in this book, as that is how she knew the city. There are a number of other Russian names throughout the book, such as the River Kura, now Mtkvari and indeed the name Zouraboff is probably the Russian version of a Georgian name.

The story draws on writings left by Marie Zouraboff, from events she related to me over the years and to some extent on my personal knowledge. Descriptions of her life in Georgia and Russia and the terrors of the Bolshevik Revolution are largely written by Marie Zouraboff herself. Unfortunately she did not complete the story, although her mind was lively up to the end and her memory had by no means faded.

She ended her days in the peaceful village of Seale, just off the Hog's Back in Surrey. But the struggles for survival, the turmoil of her life and sometimes the sheer terror of the events through which she lived are a story that I believe should be told.

Much credit goes to Gregory Gagarin, her nephew and to Gillie Rowland, her niece for their many contributions and to my wife, Charlotte McIlwraith for her patience, helpful advice and countless hours spent editing the manuscript.

# CHAPTER 1

## GROWING UP IN GEORGIA   1900-1914

Like many of my compatriots, my parents, my sister and I fled from the Russian Revolution and eventually reached Paris on the 1st May 1920 to find the taxicabs on strike. We had been reluctant to leave Russia; we had hoped that the counter-revolution would succeed and make life safe for all the peoples of that vast land so that we might return to our home. In the eyes of the Bolsheviks, our crime was that we belonged to the wrong set of people. Members of the nobility, professionals, and officers of the armed forces and of all religious bodies became enemies of Russia, their Motherland.

It was this violent conflict which formed the backdrop of my formative years. Atrocities and terror were unleashed with the advent of the Bolshevik regime, leading to civil war throughout Russia. In opposition to the Bolsheviks were the White armies who remained loyal to the Tsar. These poorly equipped, uprooted and dismayed men fought valiantly to free Russia from such unbelievable peril, but the odds were too heavy against them. They needed help from the outside world; their efforts became increasingly disorganised and the men more and more disheartened. The Allied armies during the First World War were too hard pressed with their struggles against Germany in the years 1917–1918 to pay much heed to supplications for support. Although some Allied missions were sent as assistance to the Tsar, there was little they could do to stem the misery of defeat.

My father, Nicholas Simionovitch Zouraboff, was a Privy Councillor, a senior civil servant in the Tsarist government.  He was also a General in the Tsarist army - not a fighting General, but an engineer responsible for military logistics, the construction of railways and oil and gas pipelines. He designed and built part of the second track for the Trans-Siberian Railway, which meant that tunnels and bridges along the route had to be widened to accommodate it, an enormous undertaking.

Father was born in Tiflis in 1855, the youngest of seven children. His ancestors owned camel caravans and traded in spices, textiles, precious stones and silks. They

## The Georgian Girl

travelled between the Caucasus, Iran, Afghanistan and India over the same routes probably taken by Marco Polo. Father lost both his parents before the age of five and grew up in the care of the old family nurse, who, although illiterate and of humble origin, had her charge well educated. As a young man, he travelled abroad learning French and English, then went to the University of St. Petersburg to study engineering. On his return to the Caucasus, he participated in the construction of the original Trans-Caucasian Railway and was then assigned to the Baku–Batuum oil pipeline project, which was completed in 1902. It was the longest large-bore pipeline in the world at that time, and it was in full use up to and during World War II.

My mother, Anne Marie Tollet, a French woman born in Georgia, was pretty, vivacious and twenty years younger than my father. She married him shortly after completing her convent education in France. Her family could be traced back to the French Revolution during which a young woman, whose surname was de Saint Germain, was saved from the guillotine, in the manner of the Scarlet Pimpernel, by an Englishman named Sigworth. She later married him and had two daughters, one of whom, my great-grandmother, married a Frenchman named Tollet and they lived in Lyons in France. Monsieur Tollet was a gambler. He lived on his wife's dowry until it was exhausted. He then pledged my great-grandmother on the turn of a card and lost her to two Armenians who had been sent to Lyons to look for a tutor for the sons of a Caucasian prince. She was eminently qualified as someone who had knowledge of physics and chemistry, and also of languages. Madame Tollet had to leave her children in Lyons with her sister, Madame Michallet, and make the long and hazardous journey to Batuum, where she took up the position of governess in the prince's household.

After some years, having fulfilled her duties as governess, she returned to Lyons, collected her children and went to live permanently in Tiflis. She also gathered up a selection of French clothes and opened a fashionable dress shop in Tiflis across the street from the Opera House. The business prospered, and eventually she bought a factory making soaps and candles, which were in very short supply, and it too became very profitable. In the early 1880s she bought some oil fields near Baku; however, with the primitive drilling techniques of the day, little oil was produced and her fortune was exhausted in her attempts to develop the fields, which she was then obliged to sell. The buyer was Mr. Nobel who developed more advanced drilling techniques, was able to drill deeper and eventually made his huge fortune. This result broke her heart, and she died shortly after.

Her oldest son, Ferdinand Tollet, managed the soap and candle factory in Tiflis, but died of a heart attack at the age of forty. He had three children, Louise, Michel

## The Georgian Girl

and Anne, all of whom were educated in France. Louise, who was the oldest, married and went to live in Monaco and I don't know what became of Michel. Anne, my mother, returned to Tiflis after her education and married my father - this was when he was working on the Baku to Batuum pipeline and living in Batuum. It was his second marriage, and he had a daughter, Genia, who was eight years old. His first wife had been a Russian; she had gone to the circus and shortly after, developed pneumonia and died. Because of that, none of us were ever allowed to see a circus or even to say that we would like to go to one.

My parents were married in 1893, and in 1896 my sister Elizabeth, known as Lily, was born. Four years later I arrived. Unfortunately I was not well received by my father, as he was desperate for a son and refused to see me, so I was banished to the nursery with Minnie, my English nanny. In addition to us, mother had her stepdaughter to bring up who was only ten years younger than her. The older they became, the greater the friction between them – there was too little difference in their ages and they were both strongly opinionated, so it was difficult for both of them.

Our home was just outside Tiflis. I was born there while my father was building the pipeline. We considered ourselves Russians, and Georgia as a part of Russia; that is what is understood by the phrase describing the Tsar as Ruler of all the Russias. We had a large house on the outskirts of Tiflis where lots of friends and relatives came to visit us, and where I met many important and interesting people. I was educated at home by Minnie and later by other English governesses, so I grew up speaking Russian, French and English, and by the time I was seven I spoke all three languages fluently. I have always said I used to cry in English, and it has been a very natural language for me, since I spoke it from my earliest days.

My arrival in the world was soon followed by the Russo-Japanese war of 1904/05, which was in turn followed by the 1905 Revolution. There were assassinations, bombs were thrown in public places, and many innocent people lost their lives. The uprising was subsequently quashed by the police, Cossacks and the armed forces who generally remained loyal to the Tsar. There were many arrests and deportations to Siberia. Among those deported was Joseph Stalin, who, under his own name of Djugashvili had played a prominent role in the organisation of the 1905 Revolution in the Caucasus. One of my childhood friends was kidnapped by Stalin and his gang and held for ransom - that was what he did to raise money for his activities. She was eventually returned after the money was paid, but suffering from smallpox. Luckily she recovered.

I think poor mother lived in constant fear of father's outbursts of temper, due

## The Georgian Girl

possibly to his southern blood. One morning he was in a terrible rage. "Someone has taken my pen," he yelled. In turn each family member was summoned to his study. When I was summoned, being only about 3 feet 6 inches tall, I could see that his pen had rolled under the inkstand. "You fool, why don't you look more carefully," I said. There was a tense moment of silence, and then he saw it. From that day our relationship changed, and I think we developed a certain admiration for each other.

In the years preceding the First World War, I was growing up in the narrow confines of the nursery, but with occasional travels abroad. Minnie left us to return to England when I was five. I had lessons from a series of governesses and tutors. My acquaintance with the outside world was limited to Christmas parties, and occasionally I was allowed to play with a girl of my own age who lived across the street. I saw little of my half-sister, Genia, who was grown up and married by then.

My father was against our seeing other children for fear that we might catch some dreadful illness. However, although my sister and I never went to school, we managed to have all of the childhood diseases. Our lessons were extremely patchy and at no time did my parents consider our education important. When I asked to be sent to school, my father's response was that he did not hold with learned women and as long as I acquired nice manners and had knowledge of a few languages, that was all that was needed. He ended his pronouncements by saying that I had nothing to fear since I was going to be quite pretty and wealthy enough to choose any husband I fancied. Since no one could foresee the future, I do not blame my parents for their unrealistic attitude towards our upbringing. They were merely following the received wisdom of the time.

Tiflis is a fair-sized town and the capital city of Georgia; it has a long history. Founded 1500 years ago, it was conquered and burned many times by warring Turks and Persians, together with the Moslem tribesmen of the Caucasian mountains. When in 1800 the last king of Georgia, George XII, lay dying, he took a decisive step and offered the crown to Tsar Paul I of Russia. Thus Georgia became part of Russia, and from then was ruled by a Viceroy appointed by the Tsar, although this did not extend to the warring Moslems in the mountains, the conquest of whom took the Russian armies almost fifty years to accomplish.

There was a good deal of social activity in Tiflis. Receptions were held at the Viceroy's palace; there was a state Opera House and Conservatoire, where one of the pupils was the famous singer Chaliapin. Also there were theatres, social clubs and out-of-town restaurants where one went to eat shish-kebab, watch the dancing,

## The Georgian Girl

and listen to the Zourna, an instrument played by Georgians, somewhat reminiscent of Scottish bagpipes. All this took place in exotic gardens. Many of the adults had a wonderful life before 1914 and, while watching my mother being prepared for a party or state function, I dreamt of the time when I would be getting dressed for my first ball as a debutante.

Some of my childhood recollections stand out very vividly. There were visits to my great-grandmother's factory on the outskirts of Tiflis. She was then ninety-six years old and lived with a nurse in a small house adjoining the large one where her son Henri and his family lived, and from which they managed the business for her. We were driven there in a carriage through the old oriental part of the town known as the Maidan which was populated by Tartars, Persians, Armenians and romantic-looking Arabs. The streets were narrow and overcrowded, not only with people, but with sheep and gobbling turkeys being driven to market. In the shops one could find oriental carpets, silver ornaments with black enamel designs, and silver filigree jewellery dotted with turquoise stones. There were Astrakhan furs and shops with sweetmeats like Turkish delight. Our mouths watered at the aroma of spicy foods being cooked outside on the pavement on charcoal braziers. On crossing the river Kura, which at this juncture was swift, deep and narrow as it passed through steep banks, an ancient and forbidding fortress dominated the scene.

There were sulphur baths in the Maidan of great antiquity to which we were taken by mother as a special treat. On the outside of the building were mosaics and tiles of lovely faded hues with Arabic inscriptions, and inside, in addition to mosaics and tiles, were many mirrors surrounding the baths and couches. After being bathed and scrubbed, we had lunch sent in from the pavement vendors. We always asked for *lue-la-kebab*, which we ate wrapped in *lavash*, a thin-as-paper unleavened, white bread baked on hot stones. It was a delicious meal in spite of the strong sulphur smell of the establishment.

The Tiflis season ended in early spring. A few weeks later it became too hot for us to stand the arid heat of the city and late in March we used to leave for our villa on the shores of the Black Sea, near Batuum. There the climate was semi-tropical and there were many rare flowers in our grounds. There were also palm trees and orange and lemon groves, and Cypress in profusion. Three hundred and twenty steps lined with Cypress trees swept down from the terrace in front of the villa to the rocky shores of the Black Sea. The view was magnificent - the mountains rose abruptly from the sapphire-blue sea, their lush, green vegetation snow-capped at the summit. There were deep shimmering pools where we splashed happily, before climbing onto the rocks to dry off in the boiling sun. I had a horse called Chita with whom I explored the countryside. In the evening, the nightingale sang, and our night watchman hummed to himself as he made his rounds.

I loved those days at the Green Cape, as the house was called, but we never stayed long and at the end of May, my mother took us abroad, first to a German watering resort where she took the cure – this seemed to be the fashionable thing to do - then on to Paris where we trailed round museums and to dressmakers and milliners. Sometimes, when our governess went to England for her holiday, I would be sent with her to stay with Minnie, who lived in London just off Russell Square. Minnie was very good-natured and gave me a wonderful time by indulging me, and not constantly reminding me that I should behave like a lady. We went for walks and expeditions, to the zoo in Regent's Park and to Madame Tussaud's waxworks, though I do not remember the Chamber of Horrors; this must have been omitted from the tour, as my mind was mainly filled with groups of Kings and Queens in their gorgeous clothes.

In the summer of 1914, my mother, not being well, decided to cancel her annual trip abroad and instead to follow the advice of her doctor to consult a specialist in St. Petersburg. It was arranged that she would go there late in June. My sister Lily, our governess and I accompanied her on this four-day train journey. It was hot and sticky although we travelled in the utmost comfort, occupying three compartments in the coach. Before our journey ended we heard that the Archduke of Austria, Franz Ferdinand, and his wife, the Archduchess, had been assassinated in Sarajevo by a fanatical Serb. This shooting really signalled the start of the First World War, but it was several weeks before hostilities began.

Soon after arriving in St. Petersburg, my mother went into hospital for an operation, and we were sent to stay with the Baron and Baroness Girard in Gatchina, a small town about thirty miles from the city. It was wonderful to be out of the heat of St. Petersburg and away from the rooms of the Astoria Hotel, for although it was a very luxurious hotel, it was not really appreciated by me at my age. The house in Gatchina was spacious and delightful. The grounds were extensive and there were stables, tennis courts and many dogs of all breeds. To my greatest joy, I was given a puppy, a Toy Terrier, whom I named Ricky in honour of his father. Our host's daughter, Julinka, and I were about the same age, and we became good friends. The carefree summer months went by much too swiftly, riding, playing tennis, meeting people and travelling about in a car, which was then still quite a novelty. This particular car was a little green monster with seats perched up high from the ground. There were no doors and few safety features, and one day when I was alone in the back seat, as we were going round a sharp bend I tumbled out. To

## The Georgian Girl

my great surprise the car did not stop, and I found myself alone in a dusty ditch full of nettles, watching the car vanish in the distance. Apart from some stings, I was not hurt, but vexed and apprehensive. Never had I been allowed to venture out alone and there I was on an unknown road, with no idea what to do. After what seemed a very long time and when I was in a state of near panic, I heard the roar of a noisy engine - it was the green monster. The occupants stopped the car and laughingly bundled me back in, and then drove back to the house, where I was bathed and put to bed. This upset me no end as I had been looking forward to dining downstairs on that particular evening, as Julinka's handsome young uncle, Shoura, was to be there and I had fallen madly in love with this good-looking officer from one of the Imperial Guards regiments. Shoura had no idea of my infatuation and would have been highly amused had he known. I was thirteen years old, and my romantic state must be attributed to the delightful summer and its nostalgic white nights, when the sun sets at eleven o'clock in the evening, and rises at one o'clock in the morning.

In July, I was taken to see a military ceremony, Zaria, at Krasnoe Selo. The Emperor Nicholas II was reviewing his troops, mounted on a lovely chestnut. In the pavilion nearby the Empress, their son the Tsarevitch, and their four daughters the Grand Duchesses, watched the impressive show of military might. With them was the President of the French Republic, M. Raymond Poincaré, on a State visit to Russia. I felt exhausted and a little dizzy with all the pageantry and the glaring sun beating down on the open stand where we sat. What a memorable day it was - the end of an epoch, and the end of so many things that I had taken for granted.

The dark shadow of war was sprung on me in the early hours of an August morning. The sound of a car coming up the driveway woke me, then I heard voices, and a door slammed. Julinka, in whose room I slept, jumped out of bed and ran out to the landing. When she returned and saw I was awake, she said, "It is father back from the Palace at Tsarskoe Selo. War has been declared by the Germans". I was completely miserable and wept disconsolately for a long time.

Two days later we went to see Shoura off to the front lines. His regiment was boarding a train in a siding in the nearby woods. It was a busy scene - men toiling with heavy equipment and horses being led into the boxcars - some were difficult to manage. There was a good deal of shouting and cursing. The air was hot and dusty, flies were swarming around like clouds, the trees stood drooping, and not a leaf quivered, as the laden train moved slowly away to war in the west.

# The Georgian Girl

*Tsar Nicholas II greeting the French President Monsieur Poincaré*

*The Green Cape, the Zouraboff's summer house on the Black Sea*

# The Georgian Girl

*Marie Zouraboff aged about three*

*Madame Zouraboff with Lily & Marie*

*Madame Zouraboff  
– Marie's mother circa 1904*

# The Georgian Girl

*General Nicholas Zouraboff – Marie's father*

# CHAPTER 2

## LIFE IN IRKUTSK   1914-1917

During the summer of 1914, my father was appointed General Manager of the eastern section of the Trans-Siberian Railway. His first assigment was in Harbin, where he was to negotiate with the Chinese authorities for permission to build a more direct line to Vladivostok, passing through Chinese territory, and then to supervise its construction. Although we were provided with a house in Harbin, I do not remember much of living there. I was fourteen years old and I believe we spent a lot of time visiting St. Petersburg during that year.

Father's next assignment was the reconstruction of tunnels and bridges around the shore of Lake Baikal, a distance of about one hundred and sixty miles. The original single-track line had been built in 1902, with narrow bridges and tunnels, which could not accommodate a second track. The mountainous rocky terrain, with a sheer drop into the lake, presented a major engineering undertaking as, in the first instance, a ledge to carry the track had to be dynamited out of the rock face. It was an enormous undertaking because of the size of the mountains of rock, which had to be blasted away. There were also about forty-five tunnels to be bored, and galleries had to be constructed to catch the rocks, which would otherwise have fallen onto the villages below.

We were to live in Irkutsk in Siberia, and father had gone ahead with four of our servants and the household belongings. When a house was found and all was ready to receive us, father came to fetch us from St. Petersburg, which at the outset of war with Germany had been renamed Petrograd.

My mother, still convalescing, dreaded the impending journey into the vast unknown wilderness of Siberia, away from her relatives and friends, and most of all the warm climate of the Caucasus. Our house in Tiflis, in which I was born, was closed up to await our return, but we never lived there again and I heard it said that the Bolsheviks had taken it over and used its cellars as an interrogation centre.

We left St. Petersburg early in September 1914. The new railway coach assigned

## The Georgian Girl

to father was coupled to the end of the Trans-Siberian Express. The coach looked quite ordinary from the outside, except for the full-length windows at the rear. It was painted green and a number six in brass was affixed to the door panel. On entering, one immediately saw the luxurious pale green carpets, the mahogany woodwork, the brass lamp stands and wall brackets with silk lampshades. The walls were also painted pale green. The lounge, which contained the long observation windows, was furnished with a sofa, two club armchairs in brown leather, a dining table, and two smaller tables all made in England and bought from Maples. Father's compartment had a bed, a large writing desk and chair, and a washstand. Next came mother's compartment, a smaller version of father's. My sister Lily and I shared another compartment with a double bunk, and our governess, Miss Morphet, occupied a similar one. Beyond that, a door separated us from a washroom, attendant's quarters, cupboards, a pantry, and a very modern looking kitchen. Little did we know that coach number six would later become our only home in which we would live for almost two years.

When it was time to leave for Irkutsk, father's carriage, with the observation window, was not at the end of the train as it had been, but next to last, and the Tsar's carriage was being coupled behind it. Father asked the Station Master if the Tsar was taking the train; the answer was no, but Rasputin was travelling on it. While the royal carriage was being coupled to ours, Rasputin walked onto the platform and his eyes met those of my sister who was standing some distance away. She said his glance struck her like lightning. She placed her hand on the back of her head, as her feeling was one of being 'pierced' as if by a knife. She was quickly called away by father, who made arrangements for our coach to be attached to the next train travelling to Siberia.

The journey from St. Petersburg (or Petrograd) to Irkutsk, took about six days and we soon settled down to enjoy our venture into the unknown. On the evening of the second day we reached Perm, a town at the foothills of the Urals, an unimpressive range of mountains, more like undulating hills. The next stop was Ekaterinburg, and between these two towns there was a column at the side of the railway track marking the boundary line that divided Europe from Asia.

Now before us lay Asia. The scenery was rather desolate and very flat, but here and there the land had been turned into farmsteads, which looked more prosperous than those we had hitherto seen on the European side of the mountains. The villages too seemed better kept and neater; the Izbas, built of whole wooden logs, typical of houses in Russian villages, had beautifully carved and painted window frames and porches, and the windows were curtained and had potted plants on the sills. Each of the villages had a church with a tall, onion-shaped cupola of pale green or glittering gold, which shone in the rays of the sun like a flaming torch.

The villages were mostly situated near a railway station and when a train was due the villagers would come to the platform to sell their farm produce - fruit and berries, home-made pies, roast chickens, and salted cucumbers. It was universal for stations to supply passengers with free boiling water, and all and sundry rushed with their kettles and tea pots to make tea. There was no need to hurry as the train usually stayed at least twenty minutes at each station. The more sophisticated passengers of the Trans-Siberian Express, those who had the services of a dining car, bought fruit and berries. At Perm and Ekaterinburg there were a number of small shops on the platform where one could buy precious stones from the Ural Mountains and a variety of carved and painted wooden boxes, cigarette cases, and photograph frames beautifully made by local peasants.

As our journey continued further east, I was struck by the vastness of the Siberian rivers. The Ob is particularly majestic. The train goes across by a seven span bridge, and the Ob, descending from the slopes of the Altai mountain range, disgorges itself hundreds of miles away into the Arctic Ocean. We were now travelling through the Taiga, the dense virgin forests of conifer and silver birch trees, where animals reigned: bears, wolves, the catlike lynx, sables, ermine, and mink. This was the hunting ground for the merciless fur-trappers.

On the evening of the sixth day we reached Irkutsk. The station was on the south bank of the Angara River, and the town was situated on the opposite shore. We crossed the Angara by a pontoon bridge. During the late autumn, when the river began to freeze over, the pontoon would be removed so that until the Angara was solid ice there was no possible way of getting across to the railway station. This state of affairs could last as many as fourteen days, after which one could cross by a road which was laid over the frozen river. In the spring, when the thaw set in, the same procedure took place, but in reverse.

Ivan the Terrible, in order to extend the land under his control, sent the Cossacks to Siberia to drive out the Tartars and reclaim this territory for Russia. Thus Irkutsk became a Cossack settlement in the mid-seventeenth century. This settlement grew into a trading centre with coalmines, salt deposits from the region and with tea, silks, and furs in transit from distant parts. In the nineteenth century gold was found in eastern Siberia adding more prosperity to Irkutsk and among the conglomeration of log cabins and modest wooden houses, some very elaborate dwellings were built by wealthy merchants.

A fire in 1879 destroyed most of the town, but fortunately not the Governor-

# The Georgian Girl

General's house, which had been built in 1850. It was a porticoed white mansion with imposing Corinthian pillars and it overlooked the Angara River. This mansion was built for the first Governor-General, General Nicholas Mouraviov, who later was given the title of Count Mouraviov-Amursky by the Emperor Nicholas I, for the expansion of Russian influence which he achieved over the Amur and Ussuri regions.

The house we were to live in was on Bolshoy Street. It was a single-story brick building with a semi-basement. The reception rooms faced the street; father's study, the dining room and bedrooms overlooked a paved courtyard on the north side and a small garden on the south. The outlook from the front windows was of a fairly wide tree-lined street. Directly opposite was a tallish grey fence and hidden beyond this was a large garden, the tall trees of which partly screened a grey house. We were to share this house with its owner two years later.

At an angle through our windows, we could see the pink and buff stone Drama Theatre, constructed with money contributed by the citizens of Irkutsk after the great fire. Our neighbourhood gave the impression of a pleasant village, but the Bolshoy Street away from the river became more commercial with shops and business premises. In a square nearby was an open-stall market, which did not look different to any other of its kind in the world except for the Nalim a freshwater fish from the Angara, a species completely unknown outside the region. It had an enormous liver which was considered a delicacy; also in this market, red caviar was very plentiful and cheap. In winter, when it became exceedingly cold, I was amazed to see piles of what seemed to be greyish-white cobblestones being sold by weight. This proved to be frozen milk. However, we were lucky enough to have liquid milk delivered in a heated cart to our door. The Siberian national dish is Pelmeny, minced beef wrapped in dough like a dumpling, the size and shape of a small ear. Prepared in large quantities, it was immediately frozen, ready to be eaten when required, by plunging it into boiling water, and cooking it for a few minutes. Frozen food is no novelty in Siberia; it had been available for many generations.

Vera Nicholaevna, my tutor, gave me lessons each morning; she was intelligent and charming. Her past was far from ordinary however, as in St. Petersburg at the age of sixteen, she had hurled a bomb into the carriage of an unsuspecting dignitary, and consequently spent some time in a hard labour camp in Siberia. As she was not permitted ever to return to European Russia, she settled in Irkutsk and took up teaching. I became very fond of her for she was a wonderful teacher. After lunch, Miss Morphet insisted on giving me English dictation. I am certain this was a conspiracy between her and mother, as I was all for going out for a walk at this particular hour, when the students were let out from school. After all, these first few months were very dull for me, as I knew no one of my own age. Because my upbringing was very strict, it would have been shameful had I dared to smile at a schoolboy in the street, so I boiled with rage, and fretted, to the detriment of my studies.

Snow began to fall in October. It came down relentlessly, and kept piling up until the road was at the level of our windows. I soon became accustomed to these new surroundings, and to the cold. Now we had to wear fur-lined overcoats, fur bonnets to cover our ears, together with leggings and felt boots, before venturing out of doors. It was quite a common occurrence to rush up to a total stranger in the street and rub his nose or cheeks with snow to prevent frostbite. One could detect this condition by whiteness on the affected area.

The war with Germany seemed unreal in this far-away outpost. Lily became a Red Cross nurse and went to the local hospital daily, while mother had a sewing party in the dining room twice a week, attended by a devoted band of women who made bandages and shirts for the soldiers at the front. There were also charity balls and such-like in aid of the Red Cross. News from the war-front was fairly good, and prisoners-of-war began to make their appearance in Siberia. There were thousands of them, mostly Germans and Austrians. The Austrian Empire had many nationalities, and a large proportion of their armies consisted of Hungarians, Magyars, Serbs, Croats, Czechs and Slovaks, and large numbers of them surrendered to the Russians. Some of the prisoners were employed on building tunnels and bridges round Lake Baikal.

Eventually our first winter in Siberia was over. When the thaw came, the roads turned into streams of muddy water, and in no time at all the lilac came into bloom; then the meadows became a mass of colourful wild flowers - jonquils, forget-me-nots, poppies and lilies-of-the-valley. I was given a lovely grey horse to ride; his name was Nalim, like the name of the fish with the large liver, but I could not see the connection.

My life almost came to an end one morning when Nalim shied at an oncoming motor as we were crossing the Angara by the pontoon bridge, which was crowded with people and carts. I saw the cold, swift river much too close for comfort as Nalim pirouetted and pranced about, so close to the low railing. I knew that I would have little chance of surviving a plunge into the river, as the water was icy cold even in mid-summer. I begged the stable lad, who was escorting me not to mention this episode at home and I continued my rides undeterred. I soon found that I was not alone in exploring the countryside. Beyond Irkutsk, two riders joined me – one of

## The Georgian Girl

them I knew by sight, Volodia Rassoushine. His parents were the owners of the grey house opposite ours. He was sixteen years old and had an older sister Lialia, and two younger brothers. The Rassoushines were Siberians, descended from the early settlers, and they were an interesting and talented family. Volodia played the piano very well and Lialia was good at the violin. Their mother was an intellectual and more interested in books and studies than in running the household or taking care of her children, for whom she employed a French governess. Mr. Rassoushine was often away looking after their business, which I believe was coal mining. His sister, Koka, a formidable woman, took charge of the housekeeping and ruled supreme. Koka lived alone in a flat on the ground floor, although she spent her life upstairs scolding everyone.

During the winter months, the paths in their garden were flooded, so that one could skate on the smooth surface of the formed ice. There was also an ice hill, a wooden structure thirty feet high, which supported a slope of solid ice. Steps on the side led to the top platform, from where we hurled ourselves down on individual sleighs. However, our favourite sport was to venture on skis into the wooded hills, dodging trees and other obstacles on our wild descent.

My father was often away from us working on the construction project around Lake Baikal. It was of great urgency that the second track be opened to traffic, as the war materials for the front coming from America and Japan were accumulating on the docks at Vladivostok, because of the slow progress of trains on the single track through Siberia. Sometimes father would take us along with him and we would stay on the siding in railway coach number six. On one occasion we spent a couple of days aboard the icebreaker train ferry, Baikal. She was built in England in 1895, and shipped in sections to be reassembled and launched from the shores of the lake early in the twentieth century, and went into regular service between the western and eastern shores. When fully loaded she could carry the whole of a passenger train or twenty-five freight cars. However, she proved powerless in severe temperatures, as no sooner did she break the ice, than it formed solidly again behind her. The good ship Baikal was in fact a white elephant. Her end came when she was blown up during the civil war in 1919.

The beautiful Lake Baikal is of immense depth. The shores are mostly very steep. The water is crystal clear, but very cold and menacing. It stretches for three hundred and eighty miles and is about forty miles at its widest point. The Angara flows from the south-western end of the lake, where the rock Shaman prevents Lake Baikal from overflowing into the countryside, and forms the source of the Angara River, which then flows very swiftly into the Yenisey River. Sometimes Irkutsk experiences earth tremors and everyone prays that the Shaman rock will hold fast so that Irkutsk will not be submerged in the deluge. The winter months present another hazard when the ice piles up at the entrance to the Angara. The build-up eventually mounts the riverbanks and blocks the railway lines, so the ice has to be dynamited to clear the tracks.

On one occasion, the military mission to Japan, headed by the Grand Duke George Michailovitch, was stranded at Irkutsk station for several hours, while the track was cleared of ice. My parents invited the Grand Duke and his entourage to our house for lunch. He came with his aide-de-camp Count Ilya Tatichtchev, and with the Japanese General, Prince Nakajima and his aide-de-camp. The local officials invited were the Governor General and the Military Commander of the region. It was a very formal affair. My sister greeted the Grand Duke by playing one of his favourite Caucasian tunes on the piano; Miss Morphet fell in love with the Count, who paid no attention to her, but was much taken by a miniature painted on ivory of Marie Antoinette of France, though he did not like the frame. He begged my mother to let him take the miniature, so that on his return to Petrograd he could request the jeweller Fabergé to make a more suitable frame, and to this my mother very reluctantly assented. We never saw the miniature again nor heard from Count Tatichtchev, but many months later, we were told that he was seen boarding the train at Tsarskoe Selo, in which the Imperial family were being taken into exile to Tobolsk in Siberia.

# The Georgian Girl

*General Zouraboff leaving coach number 6*

# The Georgian Girl

*General Zouraboff in full military uniform*

# The Georgian Girl

*Madame Zouraboff - circa 1910*

# The Georgian Girl

*Marie in Irkutsk aged about fifteen*

# The Georgian Girl

*Marie on Chita – circa 1916*

# CHAPTER 3

## A VISIT TO TIFLIS AND A TERRIFYING RETURN   1917

In the midst of the Christmas celebrations and the New Year of 1917, mother heard that her mother, Mme. Tollet was seriously ill in Tiflis, where she was living with her daughter-in-law in the annexe to our house. After a great deal of commotion and hysterics, mother left Irkutsk, taking me with her on this long journey back to the Caucasus to find my granny at the end of her life. She was very frail and hardly able to speak. Her last words were ominous. "My poor children! I am leaving you with great sorrow and anxiety, as you are going to see terrible things happening. There will be so much strife and bloodshed, and they will come into your houses and take your bread."

We stayed in Tiflis for a while after the funeral, and it was hard to return to the cold north. Spring was in the air here, but it would not be so in Siberia for many months. We had so many old friends to visit, but eventually we started back on the morning of 22$^{nd}$ February. Our friends came to see us off bringing flowers and sweets. The Station Master said to mother, "Your Excellency, I have to warn you that perhaps you should not leave today as there are bread riots in Petrograd and we have had no communication from there for several hours." To this, in true Gallic fashion, mother shrugged her shoulders and replied, "If there are troubles there, by the time we reach Petrograd, the police will have dealt with the disturbances."

And so we left Tiflis by train and started our hazardous journey home. On the third day we encountered the cold and bitter winter. Snow was falling and, by the afternoon, our train became stuck in a drift. After a while, as no one came to dig us out, the train crew and the more energetic passengers cleared the snow from the lines. By the time the train began rolling again we were twelve hours late. We had not yet reached Moscow, and the train crawled along all through the night and when eventually we did arrive in Moscow, late next morning, chaos reigned. This was our first shocking impression of things to come. The platform was crowded with soldiers, dirty, unshaven, ugly men, in unkempt uniforms, but armed with all kinds of weapons. They were the first wave of army deserters, and among them were sinister-looking men in black leather jackets adorned with red rosettes and red armbands, equally armed to the teeth. They stood about and held meetings, and their blood curdling speeches made us quickly return to our coach. As the train pulled out of the station, one of our travelling companions, an army officer, brought a loaf of bread for us. His tunic was torn, and one of his epaulettes hung by a thread. "They swore at me and tried to tear off my epaulettes," he said.

After four days on the train, trundling across Russia, out of touch with father and Lily, we were both stunned and apprehensive. The most frightening aspect of our predicament was the complete lack of information. Where were the police, the newspapers? Where could we get food? What was happening in the capital? Where were the Tsar and his loyal troops? From a passenger who had boarded the train in Moscow and who was a member of the Duma (Russian Parliament), we learned how the revolution had begun.

The winter of 1916/17 was exceptionally severe. Supplies of food and fuel were prevented from entering Petrograd by the disruption of the railways, which had been brought to a standstill by extreme frost and snowdrifts. Bread riots were started by a band of infuriated women, strikes followed, and masses of factory workers downed tools and marched through the streets towards the Duma, which was housed in the Tauride Palace. First the Pavlovsky Regiment, then the Volinsky Regiment mutinied and the commanding officer of the Volinsky was killed by his own men. The police were unable to quell the masses, and were soon overpowered. The fortress of Petropavlosk was stormed, and the prisoners released to join the revolution, along with other regiments of the army. From his field headquarters at Mogilev, the Tsar sent orders dissolving the Duma. The members then met, and being very much at the mercy of the left-wing socialist-revolutionaries and the newly formed Soviet of the workers and the army, formed a Provisional Government headed by Prince George Lvov. Alexander Kerensky, a young member of the Duma, and a lawyer of some repute, headed the Soviet of Workers' and Soldiers' Deputies. In the meantime, a delegation was sent to Mogilev to demand the Tsar's abdication.

We reached Petrograd at 2:00 am on a bleak and cold morning. My mother was certain that someone would meet us from the Astoria Hotel, as had happened in the past. We stood at the station entrance, overlooking Znamenskaia Square. It was deserted, except for two armoured cars, their searchlights full on, but the only sound we heard were soldiers' footsteps crunching in the snow. Our new acquaintance from the train, the member of the Duma, emerged from the station, and mother told him of our predicament. He suggested we go along with him to the Severnaia Hotel

## The Georgian Girl

across the Square. He had found a man with a sleigh for his luggage, and cheerfully piled ours on as well. The entrance to the hotel was shut and locked.

Eventually a soldier opened the door for us to enter. "What do you want?" he shouted, "Nobody is allowed in." "I am a member of the Duma and have a room reserved," said our friend. "The citizen can have a room, but what are these bourgeois women doing here? Throw them out."

The reception hall in which we stood was lit only by a flickering candle. There were no civilians there, just a group of soldiers lounging about and listening to every word. My mother said, "I am a French woman and you must find us a room, and if any harm comes to us, you will hear from the French Ambassador."

This seemed to impress them, perhaps because in support of the revolution, the Marseillaise was the song of the moment, and would be so for many more dreadful weeks to come. Eventually they let us have a room. It was very cold, as the windowpanes were riddled with bullet holes, and bits of plaster from the ceiling were spread like snow all over the floor and the furniture. We slept fitfully, fully dressed under the blankets; if only we had had something to eat!

We left Petrograd two days later on the Trans-Siberian Express. Just before leaving, we heard that the Tsar had abdicated in favour of his son, the Tsarevitch Alexis, still a child and suffering from haemophilia. Then, after further reflection, the Tsar had nominated his brother, the Grand Duke Michael, but he had refused the throne. Thus the Romanov Dynasty ended. The last Tsar of all the Russias, Nicholas II, joined his family at Tsarskoe Selo which then became their prison.

The porter disappeared with our luggage. We had lost everything, and did not even have a toothbrush. Whatever the discomfort of the journey for the next six or seven days, we had to continue, as we were anxious to know how my father and sister were faring, having had no word from them, nor any idea what was going on in Irkutsk

Most of the travellers on the train turned out to be foreigners, fleeing the country with their families, heading for the Far East, this being the only way open to getting out of Russia. Consequently the Trans-Siberian Express still maintained some semblance of comfort. Soap and toothbrushes were soon provided, so at least we could wash.

We stopped at many stations, but were afraid to leave the carriage to find food because we rather stood out by the nature of our clothes, and also because we feared that our compartment would be seized from us. In any case there was no food to be had, and very little warmth in the compartment.

Finally we reached Irkutsk, where we were met by father. He told us that he and

## The Georgian Girl

Lily had not been in too much danger, although one evening before our arrival the Commanding General of the area and his wife had escaped from their residence while the house was being ransacked by soldiers and rabble. They had sought refuge at our house, which was immediately surrounded by soldiers with their bayonets at the ready, clamouring for the General. The situation was menacing. Stanislaus, our butler, with great bravery had gone out and spoken to them. "Brothers, what is the matter with you? If you had friends in dire need on this cold night, would you not give them shelter?"

To everyone's surprise and relief, the soldiers left. Later our guests were smuggled away to a safer hiding place. After Stanislaus's brave deed, he became afraid of being arrested for defending the General. I dare say we ourselves, were not the sort of people he wanted to be associated with any longer, so after fifteen years with us, he departed with his wife, Sasha, who had been our cook. The other servants also dispersed, except for Dmitri the under-butler, and Uliana the housemaid, who was a most devoted person.

After that we moved out of the big house. The Rassoushines let us have Koka's six-room flat and she went to live upstairs with her brother and his family. My parents were arranging to send Miss Morphet back to England, but to our surprise and consternation, she declared that she was leaving us to marry a Russian. We had not been invited to the wedding, but went to see her in her new home where she seemed to be very happy. None of us ever set eyes on her husband, but Uliana, who knew something of the affair, told us that he was a schoolteacher and years younger than our poor love-struck Miss Morphet. He may have been anxious to learn English.

Father was still administering the railways, although conditions became chaotic, mostly owing to the total collapse in discipline of the railway workers. This was all happening against the backdrop of World War I, and the Allies were increasingly concerned about the break-up of the Russian front. The Provisional Government vowed to continue the war, and an offensive was being organised. The need to get military supplies through from Vladivostok was pressing. The Allies sent over military and technical personnel to supervise the flow of war material. A contingent of them were stationed in Irkutsk. There were a few British among them, and they often came to tea with us, which we all enjoyed. It must have been very boring for them to be counting the railway trucks that passed through Irkutsk, but that was all they seemed to be doing. During that time General Knox, the British Military attaché with his aide-de-camp, Captain Victor Cazelet, came to dine with us when on their way to and from Vladivostok.

## The Georgian Girl

The military offensive, early in July 1917, went well and spirits rose high. Alexander Kerensky, who had become Prime Minister as well as Minister of War for the Provisional Government, toured the front lines, encouraging the soldiers with great eloquence. The advance went well for about two weeks, but then it was halted by the German reserve troops sent to check it, discouraging our men from continuing the fight. With the help of anti-war propagandists, the Russian soldiers refused to fight and left the battlefield, taking their rifles and ammunition with them. The debacle was complete.

In Switzerland, Lenin was fretting to get back to Russia, after being exiled for political activities detrimental to Tsarist Russia. His aim was to establish peace with Germany, and to create his idealistic dream of a Communist State. The Germans agreed to help by letting him travel through Germany to Sweden in a sealed railway coach. Lenin's plans suited Germany well, as he promised to sign a separate peace treaty as soon as the Provisional Government was overthrown. Trotsky, who lived in Canada also in exile, soon joined Lenin, and together they worked to this end. "Peace! All power to the Soviets!" became their slogan.

In the meantime, the Provisional Government became anxious about the wellbeing of the Tsar and his family, who were held imprisoned in their Summer Palace at Tsarskoe Selo. Their safety was at risk, because, being so near to Petrograd, angry mobs were on the rampage more and more frequently, and the outside guards were not too reliable. Secretly on 1st August 1917, the Romanovs were transported to Tobolsk in Western Siberia.

One day, Uliana announced that she intended to get married. Her future husband, Alexis, was a soldier who had won the St. George's Cross for bravery. The wedding was to be early in September, and my parents offered to have the couple to live with us. We were invited to the wedding, which took place a few miles out of Irkutsk, at the headquarters of the groom's regiment. Mother, my sister, and I went in our carriage and were met by the Commanding Officer, who did not appear very happy about us being there, and we could not but feel apprehensive when we glanced at the soldiers who looked at us with such hostility.

After the religious ceremony, which went off quite well, we adjourned to the nearby barracks, where the reception was to be held. Having toasted the newly-weds, we were ready to leave, but no, the band struck up and everyone started to dance, so we had to join in to show our democratic spirit. After trying to follow some sort of a quadrille, we managed to get away and into our carriage for the four-mile drive to Irkutsk. The Commanding Officer insisted on escorting us and followed in his carriage through the densely wooded countryside. Suddenly, from the darkening

## The Georgian Girl

fir trees, shots were fired and as they were aimed at us, the coachman whipped the scared horses which were near to stampeding, and we got away unharmed. What happened to the Commanding Officer I do not know.

# CHAPTER 4

## OUR ESCAPE FROM IRKUTSK   OCTOBER-DECEMBER 1917

Winter was fast approaching, with frosts at night and beautiful golden days. It was early October, snow had begun to fall quietly and persistently, until tons of it covered the earth, and once again, the street was level with our ground floor windows.

The news from European Russia was scant and very disturbing. We heard of people being arrested, and no one knew their fate. The Bolsheviks were taking over towns and villages, looting, raping, and killing, spreading their communist doctrine and widening their circle of influence day by day. Many people who were not opposed to the abolition of the monarchy and agreed with the idea of a democratic government did not support them as they were too violent.

The wave of terror and chaos was gaining ground and we realised that eventually Irkutsk would fall. Father still went to his office wearing his uniform. Either he did not understand the chances he was taking or he was very courageous. One morning a delegation of railwaymen came and told him that he must relinquish his post. They were to run the railway themselves – orders from Petrograd, they said. He agreed to stay at home so as not to embarrass them, but he would not resign. Should they need advice, he said, he would gladly help them.

The Provisional Government was overthrown on 25th October. The Bolsheviks were now the rulers with Lenin fully in charge. But not all the population was prepared to succumb to his rule and a bitter civil war began in earnest. One of the first things that happened was that all the prisons were opened and the prisoners released to roam the streets in gangs, still in their prison clothes. It made it dangerous to go out. There were rumours of these men robbing passers-by, wrenching earrings from women's ears, tearing the lobes, and of other worse atrocities. Groups of soldiers appeared and with them some sinister-looking individuals in black leather jackets - they were the commissars, we were told. The telephone was cut off and there were no postmen or newspapers delivered to the door. We had no idea what was happening to our friends. What could have happened to the local government? It

## The Georgian Girl

was obvious that law and order had vanished.

The Angara river froze as the winter set in and the temperature dropped to forty degrees below zero. We were reduced to eating bread baked in our kitchen from the only flour available, which was grey-brown with bits of straw in it. Sugar had been added to make it more nourishing, but it was quite disgusting. We had little else to eat; there was some tea, but no milk, but we did have a well-stocked wine cellar and a couple of pounds of caviar, which unfortunately did not go well with the bread. On my seventeenth birthday, 10th December, we sat at the dining-room table in Koka Rassoushine's flat, drinking champagne and pretending that everything was normal. There was no birthday cake, and on this occasion, not even a crust of bread. We had guests, a few neighbours who had fled from their burning houses (two of them had not reached our house, and lay dead on the street just outside). The sniping was severe and we could hear field guns; every so often a shell would burst nearby.

At about four in the afternoon on 18th December the first shots were fired at us. We were having tea in the dining room; father was out. The shooting was sporadic, and we could not tell where it came from. Someone came to the front door. I heard Uliana go to open it and followed her. It was father; he had been running and the first thing he said was, "Close all the shutters, quickly." As he and Alexis went out to do so, a bullet came through the open doorway and I felt a thud on my head and heard something fall to the floor. The bullet had missed me by an inch and made a neat hole in the wall behind me, then spent and harmless, it had dropped onto my head. I was told it had been fired from a Colt revolver.

With the shutters closed and electricity cut off, the rooms were dark, so candles were found and lit. We decided to move to the spacious passage in the middle of the flat which ran its entire length, but had no outside walls or windows, so that we would be safe from rifle fire. We dragged mattresses from our beds and slept on the floor. No one dared to go out to see what was happening.

It must have been about two in the morning when we heard footsteps; someone was climbing the outside stairs which led to the roof. Soon after, guns opened up. The Military Academy for Officers occupied a building next to ours. The gunfire was directed at us and a shell hit one of our chimneys and exploded with a tremendous bang. Then we heard pounding on the door. Outside were the cadets with their captain, about eighty strong. The barracks were a flaming inferno, and they had decided to continue the fight from our house. The captain told us that a machine gun had been firing at them from our roof and he had thought we might be in league with the Bolsheviks. We assured him that nothing was further from the truth, but that we had heard footsteps earlier in the night. So our home now became the headquarters

## The Georgian Girl

of a detachment of loyal officer cadets.

Upon inspection, they found freshly marked footsteps on the snow-covered stairs, but the roof was abandoned, so whoever had been there had managed to escape. Our kitchen was taken over by the military. They were all young men in their teens. Their officer was giving them orders, mainly to go out and engage the enemy. The front line was the garden fence only a few yards from the house. The kitchen became an arsenal filled with rifles, boxes of ammunition, and hand grenades, but no food.

We had become resigned to living in a state of siege. I remember my mother had a toothache. She had put a bandage on her left cheek. She seemed to be in a trance, with a prayer book in one hand and in the other our toy terrier, Ricky. Father sat completely still. Occasionally he would sigh and say, "But how did this happen?"

My sister seemed to be the only one with any initiative. She kept us happy by telling funny stories, playing card games, and trying to divert our attention from the continuous sound of machine-gun fire and the moans of the wounded men who lay on the floor in the next room. There were fifteen of them, all with leg wounds, and the awful thing about it was that their legs and arms were also frost bitten. We had no medical supplies, only a small bottle of iodine, which was soon used up. After a few days of this siege, the captain came to us and told father that the situation had become hopeless and that the Bolsheviks could take our house at any time.

Father assembled us in his study, my mother, my sister, one of her friends and me. He was at his desk - a loaded revolver lay in front of him. We all understood only too well that when the Bolsheviks broke through, my father would shoot each of us and then himself. There was no other possibility. I was just seventeen years old, my whole life was before me, or so I had thought. My only crime was that I had had a privileged upbringing No one was speaking, we were just listening to the ferocious fighting, which was only yards away. As all seemed lost, Dmitri, who had been our junior butler under Stanislaus, came and spoke to father. He offered to lead us through the coal cellars to an underground passage which the Rassoushines' servants had sometimes used to sneak into town, to go to the cinema, or for secret trysts.

Dmitri was a man I hated. Not many years before, and in happier times in Tiflis, I had had a pet goose. She was very tame and a good companion and I was very fond of her. However she did not like Dmitri and would hiss at him if he came too close. One day she disappeared. No one seemed to know what had happened to her. Then a few days later at a quiet dinner with just the family, Dmitri brought in the main course, lifted the cover and revealed a beautifully roasted goose. I was sure it was my pet, and rushed from the room in floods of tears.

Now Dmitri proved to be most resourceful. He provided us with peasant-style clothing, and several bags of the type in which peasants carry their wares and livestock to market, into which we were able to pack a few of our more valuable belongings; among them was a pair of claret jugs which had been in father's study. Mother had already sewn her finest pieces of jewellery into the lining of her winter coat which she insisted on wearing, even though it was clearly not peasant garb. She said, "I am a Frenchwoman and they will not dare touch me." Although her illusions were very naïve, it showed she had great courage.

Dmitri guided us through the cellars and along a narrow, dank passageway to an exit which was close to the market square. We never saw him again. I felt in some way he had made amends for his cruel act in killing my my pet – perhaps he had not realized how devoted I was to her and felt guilty. In any case he had clearly saved our lives.

From the market square we made our way as unobtrusively as possible to the frozen river, and across it to the railway station. We could hear the shelling and see the burning buildings back in the part of town we had just left. I suppose our house had been torched, and being of wood, as were all houses in Siberia, it would have burned quickly and completely.

At the station, father found the man in charge who was well-known to us and was willing to help. Miraculously some trains were still running and he was able to get our coach attached to the next eastbound train which stopped in Irkutsk, and get us aboard. It was also a miracle that the revolutionaries had allowed the railway to continue running. I suppose it was because the Bolsheviks were able to make use of it for their own purposes.

Our coach was separated from the rest of the train and was reasonably self-sufficient, having its own bathroom and kitchen in addition to a large sitting room and three small bedrooms, so we could make ourselves quite comfortable. At each stop we could get out, stretch our legs and buy necessary provisions for the next part of the journey. However this became more and more frightening as clusters of bedraggled and menacing soldiers would threaten us, and we were fearful of being turned out of our coach, or worse; each stop was becoming something to dread.

It was difficult to decide whether to put on peasant garments, and try to blend in with the crowd, or whether it was safer to retain an air of authority and pretend to be of the commissars. The danger of seeming to be of the peasants was that others might want to share our good fortune travelling in a luxurious coach, and then of course they would realize that we were not peasants and throw us out. On balance we decided on the commissar strategy, and father wore his pistol quite openly in the hope that it would deter any challenge. It was very frightening for all of us.

## The Georgian Girl

Luckily it seemed that we were just ahead of the Bolsheviks in their move eastward. The revolution had not yet caught up with each station at which we stopped, so even though there were bands of Bolsheviks about, they were not yet fully in control. Thus we were able, by the skin of our teeth, to travel all the way to Vladivostok without any serious incidents. There our coach was decoupled and shunted into a siding adjoining the station.

# The Georgian Girl

*Vladivostok sketched by Captain Savory*

# CHAPTER 5

## VLADIVOSTOK, AND OUR ESCAPE FROM RUSSIA 1918-1920

Vladivostok remained free from Bolshevik control for the time being. On arrival, father immediately befriended the stationmaster who introduced him to many other refugees, and soon we were receiving callers from the town and from the Military Missions from various foreign countries. In a short time my sister and I were in a whirl of social activity centred on the British delegation opposite the railway station, and we were invited to many receptions and balls there. Somehow we managed to put together suitable dresses - mother worked miracles with whatever she could find, including curtains, sheets and tablecloths. Not only did she make wonderful clothes, but she taught me dressmaking, a skill which served me well throughout my life.

We had a lot of fun in Vladivostok. During the day there were parties on the beach and excursions to the Royal Navy ships, to which we were invited as guests. I spent my time working on my suntan and enjoying the company of the naval officers. I had never learned to swim and one day, thinking I should, they took me to a lagoon and threw me into the water. It was a terrifying experience for me and I sank to the bottom, well out of my depth. As I came up for the third time, one of the young officers, Alan Scott-Moncrieff, jumped in and pulled me to shore. I was miserably cold and on my big toe was firmly attached a large crab, which did not want to let go.

I made several friends among the young officers, among them Alan, who had saved my life, and later in 1919, Reginald Savory and Rusty Riviere both Captains in the British Army. I fell in love with Alan, although at the time he probably had very little idea of it.

Meanwhile father had been trying to arrange a passage for us out of Russia, but the few ships sailing were requisitioned by the military, and no space was available for civilians. It was a desperate situation because the White Army resistance under Admiral Kolchak, although starting out with great optimism, deteriorated to the point of complete collapse and the partisans, who supported the revolution, became very menacing as the Bolsheviks were extending their control of Russia. On 30th January 1920 we had no idea that danger was imminent and had gone to our railway coach and settled down for the night. We were woken at 2:00 in the morning by someone banging on the door. The unexpected callers were Captain Riviere and Captain Savory. They told us to hurry to get dressed and to come with them to safety as the Bolsheviks were advancing on Vladivostok and would be there within four hours. They took us to the residence of General Sir Alfred Knox, who had by then left Russia, but Colonel Charles Wyckham was our host and we were made most welcome there. It was a great relief and an honour to be under the protection of the Union Jack. Safety was something we had not experienced for over two years.

We remained in the General's house for about three weeks, whilst in the town there was a complete breakdown of law and order and many of our friends were arrested and imprisoned. All of our belongings were stolen from our coach, but fortunately we had taken our silver and jewellery with us. Everyone was trying to get away, but ships were even less available than before and few people were able to leave. Eventually our kind British hosts managed to persuade the captain of a Japanese freighter to take us aboard. It was sailing to Trieste carrying about a thousand Italian and Czechoslovak troops, all released prisoners of war. The Captain agreed to take my parents, my sister, me and my little dog Ricky, from whom I would not part. We were allocated the lamp room.

For the last week or so we had noticed a Bolshevik guard posted at the gate of the General's house. We wondered how we could ever get away without his knowledge, as there was little doubt he was there to shoot us, but when the time came for us to leave, the soldier was enticed to the kitchen to drink vodka and he did not notice our departure. As we left the house, mother reached down and opened her suitcase. She took out the pair of silver-mounted cut-glass claret jugs. One she gave to Rusty Riviere and the other to Reggie Savory in appreciation of what they had done for us. It was quite certain that we would not have survived without their help.

We set sail on 20th March 1920 in an old and rusting ship named *England Maru*. The lamp room in the extreme stern of the ship was just a storage place, damp and dark and rather horrid. I was frightened and very cold, lying fully dressed on a wooden bunk with a straw mattress and half a dozen army blankets over me. It was pitch dark in this iron box. I was not alone which was a comfort - occasionally I heard my parents talking in their bunks below and my sister moving about. I think we were all too scared and cold to be seasick or to care much about anything.

On the second night out we were tossed about by a violent storm, which I heard being referred to as a typhoon. The ship would plunge into a trough and the stern

## The Georgian Girl

rise out of the water, exposing the screws which spun in the air with a deafening whine; then the stern would come crashing down into the water with a tremendous bang, like the boom of an explosion, which reverberated throughout the ship. Huge waves came angrily over the superstructure in which we were trapped, all of us praying that we would not get washed away. We waited. There is a stage in fear where one becomes completely numb and calm. It takes a few hours to reach that stage, but it is a great relief to get there and to become detached, even though one's senses remain keen. I think one becomes past caring what happens. Whether or not we survive becomes immaterial, just so long as the ordeal eventually ends.

As the journey progressed, we ran out of wood to heat the small stove installed for our comfort by the kind people of the Military Mission in Vladivostok, who had also provided the blankets and straw mattresses. The darkness was terrifying. We had no food as it was expected that we would eat with the contingent of Italian troops on board. This was made impossible since the troops were only interested in sex with Lily and me, and were quite unable to accept refusal. Even though we forfeited our meals in their company, they would seek us out and aggressively force their attentions on us. It was then that my sister and I became chain-smokers. We used lighted cigarettes as weapons to repel the more overt attempts at rape, much to the chagrin of the ship's doctor who came to us and begged us not to give him so many cases of burns to treat.

It was a terribly long journey - I do not recall just how long. After we had passed Formosa and reached the South China Sea, the storms subsided and it became much warmer until we were even able to go on deck from time to time, protected only by our supply of cigarettes, although by then word had got round and the men left us alone. The *England Maru* passed through the Indian Ocean, and eventually reached the Gulf of Aden and the Red Sea. Under any other conditions it would have been most interesting, but under these circumstances, in constant terror of being raped or of having our few possessions and our jewellery stolen, it was agonizing. It was a great relief when we passed through the Suez Canal and into the Mediterranean Sea, and an even greater relief when we finally reached Trieste. I have never been so delighted and relieved to be once again on dry land.

Father, who had always travelled in style on the railways, and to make up for the appalling journey we had just endured, bought first class tickets for us all on the Orient Express to Paris. For that glorious day it seemed as if life had returned to normal.

# The Georgian Girl

*Marie Zouraboff aged about 18.*   *Reginald Savory in Vladivostok*

*Claret Jug given to Captain Savory in Vladivostok.*

# CHAPTER 6

## LIFE AS REFUGEES IN PARIS   1920-1922

On arrival in Paris the taxis were on strike. However, father was well known at the Ritz where he had stayed many times, and they immediately sent a car to collect us from the station, so we were able to stay in pampered luxury for a few more weeks. We dined at the best restaurants, and thoroughly enjoyed the many pleasures of life in Paris. It seemed that all of mother's relatives came to welcome us, but they also expected to be lavishly entertained.

Of course our money could not last for long at that rate of spending. Mother sold some of the more valuable pieces of jewellery she had sewn into the linings of her coat back in Russia. She was in her element as the grand hostess, and seemed oblivious of the precarious future we were facing. Father still clung to the belief that the rebellion in Russia would soon be put down, and that we would be able to go home. Nonetheless, he must have understood that this possibility was fast receding, especially when we started to hear rumours of the murder of Tsar Nicholas and his family, so he tried to justify these extravagances by entertaining some of his engineering contacts in the hope of being offered suitable employment. After all, as one of the world's leading civil engineers he had been personally invited by the French Government to the opening of the Eiffel Tower in 1899, and although an old man now, he had an enviable reputation as a railway engineer, and felt sure he could find a senior engineering post in France.

As the money started to run out, we left the Ritz and moved into a pension which had been highly recommended to us. It was just off the Champs-Elyseés at 18 rue Clément Marot and it is now known as the Hotel Franklin D. Roosevelt. It was then owned by the Ochs family, who greeted us warmly on our arrival. Father paid them for three months in advance, which set our minds at ease and gave us a short period of security. I think that we were all now beginning to realise how desperate our situation was, and although at this time in 1921, we were still able to live quite comfortably, and to entertain and to visit the opera occasionally, I know my father

## The Georgian Girl

worried about how to support his family over the longer term, and he did what he could to find work for himself and for Lily and me. Refugees are nowadays entitled to various benefits from the State, but no such welfare systems existed at that time, and when money ran out there was no safety net. Unemployment throughout Europe was high after the end of World War I, exacerbated by servicemen returning home, young men who naturally had better prospects than us. In addition Paris was the preferred refuge for White Russians, and there were therefore plenty of other people like us looking for work.

At the pension were many other foreign visitors on long-term stays. Among them was Ian McIlwraith, who had just come down from Oxford University to follow in the footsteps of his father Sir Malcolm McIlwraith, an eminent international lawyer of the day who was legal adviser to the Khedive of Egypt. Ian was desperately trying to live up to his father's wishes and to obtain a French law degree. However, he had no ear for languages, and was struggling to keep up with his studies. He took an immediate shine to Lily, although he was a few years younger than her, but when she spurned his advances he turned his attention to me, and we often spoke together of his beloved England, for which he was deeply homesick, and where I had spent some happy times as a child with my nanny, Minnie.

Lily was already interested in Prince Gregory Gagarin, known as Gushka, who had made a spectacular escape from a Bolshevik firing squad in St. Petersburg and like us was a refugee in Paris. As a young cavalry officer, Gushka had served at the front against the Germans in World War I in the Hussars of the Guards, the Tsar's own regiment, until the disintegration of the Tsarist armies in 1917. After the war he returned to his family's estate near Pskov in northern Russia. The peasants had been restless, but he won their respect by succeeding in selling their flax to the British government. However, the jealousy of the Bolshevik authorities in the area led to his unexplained arrest. He was kept in jail until a petition from the peasants was received asking for his release. This apparently infuriated the Bolsheviks, who then decided to get rid of him. On the 6th September 1918, Gushka and two cellmates were taken out to be shot. Guarded by an army officer, a commissar and six soldiers, all of whom were heavily armed, the three were marched toward the Porchof cemetery where they were to dig their own graves before being executed. Gushka decided he would not die without at least trying to escape. There was a chance at the first crossroads, but he lost his nerve - it is amazing how much a few extra minutes of life can be worth. However, as they approached the cemetery gates he realized that once inside his chance to escape would be irretrievably lost.

As the guards were turning to open the gates, Gushka swung the shovel he had

## The Georgian Girl

been given to dig his grave, knocked two of the soldiers to the ground and ran. He had no idea where he was going, and he could hear the guards running after him, and shots being fired. As he was flinging off his jacket to enable him to run faster, two bullets hit him, one merely causing a flesh wound, but the other hitting him in his hand, which shattered it and caused him terrible pain. Darting into a narrow street, he realized too late that it was a dead end, and that there was a brick wall at the end, which must have been at least eight feet tall. Brimming with adrenalin, Gushka managed to get over it, only to collapse and lose consciousness for a moment on the other side. When he came to, he could hear the guards saying to each other, "Where has he gone? He could not have got over that wall, no man could." Eventually they left and Gushka went into hiding, and with the help of friends made his way to Kiev and then to Odessa. There he joined the French army which was fighting the Germans and for this he eventually received the *Croix de Guerre*.

Lily became an apprentice beautician at Elizabeth Arden, selling body and face creams to the rich of Paris, and she and Gushka were married somewhere on the Champs-Elyseés in February 1921. A few months later Lily found she was expecting a baby and late in 1921 the couple moved temporarily to Wiesbaden in Germany, because Gushka happened to have been born in France and any son of his also born in France was liable to be conscripted into the French military upon reaching the required age. Clearly this was to be avoided if possible. On 22nd February 1922, a boy, Gregory, was born and a few months later the new family returned to Paris to join my family in the pension.

In these difficult times, all of father's erstwhile engineering colleagues abandoned him. Then some French relatives advised him to deposit his remaining money in a certain bank which they assured him was very secure and was offering a higher rate of interest than others. This way there would at least be a steady stream of income coming in on a regular basis on which we could live. Six weeks later the bank was declared insolvent and he lost everything. I have never forgiven my French relatives for their trickery. In the end, father, then in his seventies, was offered a job as a door-to-door salesman selling vodka primarily to other Russian refugees. He remained cheerful through all of this, but it must have been deeply humiliating and his inner turmoil must have been immense.

Meanwhile I took work looking after the children of wealthy visitors to Paris, mainly Americans, while they were shopping or out for the evening. I was probably one of the world's first paid babysitters. Among the Americans for whom I worked, was the Hodges family. Arthur Hodges and his wife Polly and fifteen-year-old daughter, Julie, were staying in Paris with his brother Captain John Hodges, who

## The Georgian Girl

though an American, had served with the British Mission in Vladivostok and was now married to a French woman, Madeleine, and living in Paris.

Arthur Hodges was one of those wealthy Americans who lived more or less permanently in Europe. However Polly, who was his fourth wife, preferred to live in America and wanted to bring up Julie there, so they decided to return to the United States in 1922, and asked me to accompany them as governess to Julie and as their housekeeper. Although I hated the thought of parting from my family, it seemed the best opportunity available, and we all agreed that I should go. Also I felt it was an adventure not to be missed, and of course the money on offer was much more than any of us could have hoped for in France. So it was decided: just as Gushka and Lily returned to Paris with their new baby, I left my family for the first time in June 1922 to sail to New York.

# CHAPTER 7

## NEW YORK 1922-1925

Arriving by ship for the first time in New York is truly exciting. At that time, in 1922, there were not many skyscraper-cities, although nowadays they are a common sight. As we sailed past the Statue of Liberty and I saw the skyline of Manhattan for the first time, I experienced a rush of feeling, a sense of the vitality of the place and of a new beginning for me. I found it difficult to hold back tears of joy and relief at putting so much distance between myself and the terrible time of our escape from Russia.

The last day on board had been a round of parties and farewells, with a place at the captain's table for our final dinner, continuing with drinks and dancing until the early morning. Then we turned in to catch a few hours of sleep before being escorted by tugs up the Hudson River and into our berth on the island of Manhattan.

Immigration inspection was a nightmare I prefer to forget. I remember an interminable wait in a long line followed by a lengthy interrogation into the reasons for my escape from Russia, and how I expected to support myself in America. Eventually, based on the affidavits provided by Arthur Hodges, I was passed as fit to reside in the United States for up to a year while employed by him, with the possibility of extending the year to a second and even a third one. I found out that Arthur Hodges had also been grilled as to why he was not employing an American as his housekeeper, but he successfully persuaded the authorities that it was not possible to find an American who could also teach their daughter both French and Russian.

Our first night in New York was spent at the Waldorf Astoria. I found the noise and excitement of the city overwhelming. Sirens rang out from emergency vehicles almost continuously and I thought New York must be burning to the ground, or that there was an enormous crime wave hitting the city, perhaps murder on every block. I even wondered if the Bolshevik revolution had followed me to America. Needless to say, I slept very little.

# The Georgian Girl

After a sumptuous breakfast at the hotel, we departed in a bright yellow taxicab to Pennsylvania Station for our train to Montclair, New Jersey, a journey of about sixty miles. Of all the many railway stations I had seen, Pennsylvania Station was the most magnificent. It had a marble floor and shops around the concourse, all brightly lit and welcoming, a great contrast to Russian and most European stations, which in 1922 were usually dirty, noisy, and full of smoke, places where you would be lucky to find an edible sandwich or a mug of tea. Our American train was also a contrast to the splendid Victorian style of first-class European rolling stock, being very sleek, though it was equally comfortable and spacious; the two levels of seats, a few steps either up or down from the corridor particularly fascinated me. Over the next three years, I took the same train frequently, and grew very fond of American railroad sounds, which were also quite different to the ones I was used to in Europe, due I believe to the way the rails were laid.

The Hodges had rented a large house surrounded by farmland. My first impression as we drove there was that everyone was car crazy: it was the day of the Model T Ford. Most of the roads were apparently unpaved country lanes and trails of billowing dust followed each passing car. We had a neighbour, Mr. Bird, who had the latest Italian import, a bright red two-seater Alfa Romeo. He used to commute every day to his office in New York, driving at great speed. Ducks, geese, and children scattered at his approach, which was always forecast by a great roar, and followed by the usual enormous plume of dust.

As I became more used to living in the United States, and more confident, I started to venture into New York. At first I went with Mr. Bird, but then I began to take the train on my own. The excitement of the bustling city and the pace of everything gradually became less overwhelming. I grew more used to the sight of skyscrapers, yet they were always thrilling and extraordinary to see, and the air, coming straight off the Atlantic, has been described as like champagne. Money was short as I had only my wages supplemented by what I made babysitting. I used to eat at the Automat, a wonderful American invention; plates of food were displayed in a bank of glass-fronted lockers, and one's choice could be got by payment of a coin in the appropriate slot; staff would then replenish the dish from behind. A hot dish could be obtained for a quarter (25 cents) and a piece of pie for a dime (10 cents).

It was a wonderful time to be in America, especially where I was, in and around New York. Fortunes were made overnight, and seemed to be within the grasp of almost anyone. Businesses were thriving, spurred on by countless innovations. The New World had released a great surge of creative energy from its immigrant people, who had been held back until now by the hopeless poverty of their previous lives. This was the age of the mass-produced car, the vacuum cleaner, the radio and the refrigerator; the art of door-to-door salesmanship was born and developed to extraordinary heights. Everyone wanted the latest gadgets, and the banks had plenty of money to lend. It was a time of tremendous optimism when America seemed to have discovered the key to wealth creation and the good life for everyone. The stock market could only go up and people were urged to borrow all they could to buy shares. Of course we now know that this could not go on forever, but at that time I remember the earnest belief that it could and would. With this optimism I also remember great generosity, for many people wanted to share their good fortune. I have no recollection of greed, but I suppose there must have been some.

However, many problems were bubbling under the surface. There was a lot of drunkenness, both before and after prohibition was passed into law in 1920. With prohibition came a huge increase in violent crime. Luckily, as an employee of the Hodges and living in an affluent suburb, I was sheltered from most of this, but reading newspaper accounts of lawlessness on the streets made me nervous. I had seen things like this before in Russia, where a desperate underclass had suddenly been joined by a mutinous army to bring about a revolution.

New York was a Mecca for Russian refugees. Long Island and particularly Seacliff and Glen Cove were the areas favoured by those who had international wealth, such as the White Star ship owners, the line which later merged with Cunard. They hosted some very grand parties and I was invited to many of them. My brother-in-law, Gushka, had also come to New York in June 1922, and he had begun to teach riding to rich New Yorkers - in Russia he had been known as an excellent horseman.

Meanwhile the Hodges decided that after all they preferred life in Europe, and in 1925 started to make plans to find a suitable house in England. Perhaps I would have liked to remain in America, but the choice was not mine. My visa had been extended for a third and last time, and once the Hodges left I would have no sponsor and no employment and could not stay. In the event, I was more than happy to accept an offer to continue as their housekeeper in England as it meant I would be nearer my family who were still in Paris.

# The Georgian Girl

*House in Montclair, New Jersey rented by Arthur Hodges*

# CHAPTER 8

## ENGLAND AND MARRIAGE  1925-1927

Arthur Hodges leased Turweston House in lovely unspoiled countryside on the borders of Buckinghamshire, Oxfordshire and Berkshire. It was a glorious spot in the middle of hunting country. We arrived there in the winter of 1925, much more damp and dreary than winter in Siberia, with hardly any sunshine. I kept myself busy looking after Julie and doing some embroidery, coupled with long walks over the surrounding fields. I had plenty of time to reminisce about life in Russia and my thoughts often turned to the exciting time in Vladivostok among the chivalrous young British officers who had made life fun, even though we were terrified for the future. I wondered whether I would meet any of them now that I was in England.

As newcomers to the village, some of the neighbours came to call on us and in turn we received invitations from them. In particular I became good friends with the Lucases (Mr. Lucas was known as Tiddly and was the Master of the local hunt, but I do not remember Mrs. Lucas's Christian name). They lived almost next door with their son and two daughters of about my age, and they were a kind and generous family. One of their daughters, Joan, took me under her wing and made sure that I was invited with her to all the debutante parties. Although I was slightly older and much more experienced than these young people I was pleased to be accepted so readily by them.

At that time, if one wanted to enter society, it was necessary to receive an invitation to a garden party at Buckingham Palace and to be presented to the King and Queen. Joan had received an invitation, and somehow one was also obtained for me. The next few months were delightfully spent looking for suitable gowns for us to be presented in. When the day arrived, we drove to London to the Savoy Hotel, and there we got dressed, and set off for the Palace. I don't remember very much about the ceremony, except Queen Mary saying that she hoped my escape from Russia had not been too awful, and that I would be happy in England, words I have always cherished. My task then was to back away from the King and Queen, making

## The Georgian Girl

sure never to turn my back on them, while at the same time being careful not to trip over my long dress.

Ian McIlwraith, who had given up his studies in Paris, had now returned to England and came to call on me at Turweston. Although I was not terribly interested in him and found him a rather gauche escort to the parties to which we were invited, he was a link with my time in Paris, and a pleasant enough companion. At one of these parties the Prince of Wales was present and he began to make it clear he found me attractive. I was not absolutely sure how I should react to his attention, but the people I was with, seeing my predicament, joined us and tactfully drew me away, saying I should steer clear of him. We left the party quickly; obviously they knew that he had a bit of a reputation for that kind of behaviour.

As the months rolled by and as Joan became more involved with her dashing young pilot officer, Tony Coke, I started to rely emotionally more and more on Ian, much to his delight. Shortly after Joan and Tony became engaged, Ian asked me to London to meet his father. Sir Malcolm McIlwraith was a brilliant lawyer but a difficult man; I believe his wife, who had died a few years earlier, did not find him a sympathetic husband. I later learned that when he had been working as legal advisor to the Egyptian government in the 1890s, he had offered to resign in exchange for a generous pension. A newspaper account of the day related that others working in his department did not want to give him the chance to change his mind and told the messenger to run very fast with the letter of resignation, which he did, so much so that he fell and broke his leg, for which he claimed compensation. I believe the letter was nonetheless delivered in time.

I went with Ian to a terribly formal lunch at 36 Stanhope Gardens. There were twelve at the table. I remember Ian's sister Enid, whom I rather liked, but the others seemed terribly oppressive. They wanted to know why we had had to leave Russia and seemed to imply that it must have been our own fault that the Russian people had overthrown the Tsarist regime. Somehow I managed to answer politely, and finally, when the meal was at an end, Ian's father turned to him and said, "She'll do." At that point I seemed to be engaged to Ian and I am still not sure whether I should have said no. I was fond of Ian, but I must admit that I was becoming rather practical, and marriage to someone well connected gave me the prospect of security.

Our engagement was announced, and we were to be married on 10th September 1927 in Turweston church, with the reception to be held afterwards at the house. There followed an extremely busy time with many trips to London to have my wedding dress fitted, and to go to the round of parties to which Ian and I were invited. I remember Julie and I trying to learn the Charleston, the latest dance craze, in her bedroom, with two hardback chairs for partners. It was all very jolly and Joan and Tony who were always at hand became very close and stalwart friends.

On the day, I was driven the very short distance in great ceremony to St. Mary's church, and there, in spite of a lot of nervousness and fumbling with the ring, we became man and wife. Afterwards we all returned to Turweston House for the reception. Arthur and Polly Hodges were very generous – they had unofficially acted as my parents for the past five years, and I will always be grateful to them. For the reception they pulled out all the stops and gave us a tremendous party, including an opportunity to dance the Charleston. As we left I threw my bouquet into the crowd of guests and, as I hoped, it was caught by Joan. Then we set off in Ian's rather rickety motor car, a Morris, which rattled more than usual because of the old tin cans which had been attached to the bumper.

Although nowadays Devon may not seem very far from Buckinghamshire, the journey was long and arduous, due partly to the state of the roads, but mostly to the rather unreliable state of the car which insisted on boiling over each time we came to a slight incline. Our tempers were therefore somewhat frayed by the time we reached the guesthouse which was quite modest and by the side of a fairly busy road, although it sat on top of a bluff and had a magnificent view of the sea. The meals were disgusting, but Ian would not let me complain. He said it was not English to complain and that in any case, the beer was very good. The window of our bedroom overlooked the road. One afternoon, while we were doing what honeymooners do, a double-decker bus made an unscheduled stop just outside the window, and the upstairs passengers had a very clear view of us. Ian was furious. He thought they should have looked the other way. As the bus moved on we could hear them cheering.

All in all, our stay was really quite pleasant. I love the sea and the Devon coast was quite unspoilt in a very English and rather delightful way and I took the opportunity to get out my watercolours and to paint the seascape, while Ian tried to make friends with the publican.

We tried to get out each day to explore the countryside and to find somewhere to eat a more appetizing lunch. On one such occasion, we had driven down to a tiny fishing village on the north coast which was approached by a long and winding dirt road. It was a most romantic spot, and we found a little café where they understood how to cook the local catch, and we had a delicious lunch. After a lazy stroll along the shore, it was time to set off on our return journey. Would the car take us up the dirt road? It would not. As much as Ian tried, it would not budge. As a dutiful wife, I offered to get out and give it a push. With me pushing and Ian gunning the engine, which covered me in a cloud of black soot, the car began to move. I ran to get in but could not quite catch up. As the car disappeared round the next corner, I felt sure Ian would stop for me, but no, he doggedly carried on to the next corner and the next for about half a mile, to the very top of the hill.

I'm afraid I was not at all understanding of his reasoning that if he stopped he would be unable to start the car again, so the rest of the day was spent in moody silence. However, I should not complain - Ian was very attentive, and did his best to show me the English way of doing things. And I must say that I have always loved Devon, the countryside and the people. It has a feeling of seafaring about it, which I have always found most attractive.

It was a shame that we never returned to that delightful village, but we did find other places where the food was quite good. I was quickly learning that in England, one has to be extremely careful in choosing food or accommodation. It can be very nice or absolutely awful, and without some inside knowledge it is hard to tell which it is likely to be. I suppose a personal recommendation from a close friend is the safest approach.

# The Georgian Girl

*Turweston House 1925*

*Marie in grounds of Turweston House*

The Georgian Girl

*Presentation at Buckingham Palace.*

# The Georgian Girl

*Marie aged 26 in Paris*

*Ian McIlwraith in the car in which he & Marie drove to Devon.*

# The Georgian Girl

*Marie with Nicky in London 1931*

# CHAPTER 9

## THE 1930S AND THE LEAD UP TO WORLD WAR II

We drove back to London and moved into our new flat at 14 Leinster Gardens. It was small and rather dark, but close to Kensington Gardens, where I used to walk almost every day. My days in London as a newlywed were busy and eventful and generally happy. I had my circle of friends from Turweston who frequently came to town, and we went to parties and the theatre. As a good wife, I did my best to entertain Ian's associates and to help him with his career as a young solicitor. His father seemed to take rather a shine to me, and I was summoned from time to time to his dinner parties, and even to accompany him on his walking tours in the Swiss Alps. Although it was all done in great luxury, I found him a more and more tiresome man, and my excuses became rather more frequent.

Ian was working for the law firm Archibald. It was in Paris and London and therefore probably one of the world's first international law practices. The founding partner, Archibald, was a great friend of my father-in-law, who I believe had helped him open a branch in Paris. So the firm owed him a favour, and took on Ian to do his Articles there. After we were married, Ian was still receiving the salary of a junior even though he had been with the firm for almost five years. He began to feel resentful and perhaps partly due to my urgings, demanded to be made a partner. Unfortunately Archibald had no intention of doing so, and felt that he had fulfilled his obligation to Sir Malcolm, and so Ian set out to find another job. Over the next few years he had several positions, but for one reason or another he ended up quarrelling with all his employers.

It was at about that time that Ian was thinking of joining a lodge of the Free Masons, I had no idea what that was all about, but had heard that it might help open some doors to his career. In fact I rather urged him to try it. In the event Ian did become a Free Mason and I believe it did help him, but not until much later.

Then I became pregnant and it was not a happy experience for me. I suffered terrible morning sickness which frequently lasted all day. I couldn't eat and was

## The Georgian Girl

actually confined to bed for several months. My doctor was not as sympathetic as I would have liked (few were in those days) and I felt terribly alone in a foreign country. I knew that Ian had his own problems, but he just wasn't around very much, and was not much help when he was. My only source of comfort was my friend Joan. She was always in good spirits and cheered me up no end. Her young husband, Tony, was also great fun and they took me out for lunch or to the cinema whenever I felt up to it.

Finally, in May 1931, I was trundled off to a nursing home on Sunderland Avenue and after being examined and prodded, was abandoned for the night. Ian, as captain of the Law Society Cricket Club, was playing an away match, so he was gone for two days. I knew I was ready to give birth, but the staff at the nursing home would hear nothing of it. At about 3 am it all happened. No one was around, but my yelling finally brought a nurse running and the doctor was summoned. When he arrived, I handed my baby to him. Nicky was born on 31st May 1931 with no medical help. I was torn and bleeding. It was not an experience I intended ever to repeat.

A week later I returned with my baby to Leinster Gardens and was introduced to a nanny whom Ian had hired. From then on I rather took a back seat and tried to regain my health. Nanny used to take the baby in his pram for outings to Kensington Gardens - sometimes I would go too, and gradually my health returned and I began to feel that we had become a little family. Joan, who was a constant companion to me, announced at about that time that she was pregnant and looked to me for advice and support. I did my best to be helpful and left out all the worst parts. Of course it was a great joy to me to have a little son and I tried to be a good mother, but really I had no idea how to go about it, and followed Nanny's advice in most things. I remember singing Russian lullabies to him and speaking in Russian, but Ian was terribly upset and said it would confuse the boy and delay his ability to talk. I hoped he would grow up fluent in several languages as I had, but it was not to be.

When he was about four months old, we took the baby to be christened at Walton-on-Thames. I don't remember why that particular church was chosen; it was all arranged by Ian and Nanny. Joan was there as godmother, and so was Julie Hodges. He was christened Douglas Malcolm Nicholas; it all seemed so pompous and from the first I called him Nicky.

During this time, I received the news that my father had cancer and was not expected to live much longer. I made a quick trip to Paris on the boat train and managed to see him for the last time. He tried to be cheerful, but the last few years of his life had taken a terrible toll and he was desperately worried as to what the future held for us all, especially for my mother. Some months later, in 1932, father died and

## The Georgian Girl

was buried in the Russian Cemetery just outside Paris.

Then one evening, out of the blue, Ian came home looking very pleased with himself, and announced that he had bought into a partnership with another solicitor. He said he felt he could be really successful if only he could work in his own way as an equal partner, and now he had seized the opportunity. This seemed wonderful news and I started to ask him about the firm and its prospects. Only then did he tell me that the partnership was in Hull in East Yorkshire, and that we would be moving there.

At first I was furious. Ian had not discussed this with me; it was presented as a fait accompli. It would leave me hundreds of miles away from the circle of friends that I shared with Joan and Tony, and away from London, where I had made contact with other Russian émigrés, most notably two of my childhood friends Julinka and Angela. I knew I would have to start all over again making friends, hundreds of miles from London, where I now felt reasonably at home, without the help and support of Joan and Tony. Ian did not seem to understand this, and insisted that Yorkshire people were lovely and that I would soon have a wide circle of friends there. I was not so sure.

We went to live in Brough, a tiny village close to the River Humber not far from Hull. Ian had rented a cottage with a large garden. I quickly found this part of England, the East Riding of Yorkshire, even more provincial than I had feared. The neighbours, although I am sure they meant no harm, would point their fingers at me and say, "There goes the foreigner." It was ghastly! The climate was dreadful - if it wasn't raining, there was a thick damp fog coming off the River Humber limiting visibility to a few feet. Nicky, who had been quite a robust baby, became very sickly and started to have eating problems.

Then my sister began writing long and complaining letters about the burden of looking after mother, and suggesting that it was my turn to keep her. I was feeling rather depressed in general, and thought that having mother with me might be quite helpful, and I managed to persuade Ian to agree to it, although really he was not at all enthusiastic. Finally he acknowledged that she would be good company for me and might help me cope with the monotony of everyday life.

And so my mother came to live with us and we fell into a routine. There was a lovely garden with the cottage and whenever the sun came out, I would work in it or do some watercolour painting. We had a little dog called Chips who adored Nicky but bit everyone else in sight including the postman, as a result of which he refused to come to the door unless Chips was locked into the house. One day when Chips was locked in and the postman arrived, the dog got so excited that he jumped

## The Georgian Girl

through the closed window shattering the pane of glass. After that the post was left each day at the bottom of the drive for me to collect.

After a year or two, Ian's partnership turned into a disaster. It was becoming clear that the books had been cooked and that the business had never made a profit and never would. We had no social life, no friends within reach, and I felt unsympathetic to Ian in his plight. Mother was another mouth to feed on a very limited budget, and on top of all this Ian had an affair with the vicar's wife. I begged him to return to London, but he wouldn't hear of it. He felt an obligation to the solicitor who had swindled him and who was suffering a slow death as a result of having been gassed in the war. He was also terrified of admitting to his father that he had made yet another bad start, and had lost the money which I suspected he had borrowed from him. He insisted on staying on in the vain hope of salvaging something from the partnership. But I had had enough. I took mother and Nicky to London, as much for his survival as for my own.

In the 1930s, there was a lot of building in progress in London, and I took a flat in a brand new block in Fulham. We were the fifth tenants to move into West Kensington Court. Soon afterwards Nicky became very ill. He had all the childhood diseases quite severely, and also developed abscessed teeth and septic tonsils. There were no antibiotics at that time, and septicaemia was usually fatal. He was rushed to hospital for a tonsillectomy - the operation was very difficult and his life hung in the balance for three days. Only then was I able to visit him, and the surgeon took me aside and told me that I must not let him cry, because it could cause a haemorrhage which would probably kill him. Somehow he survived and I took him home to the little flat and gradually nursed him back to health. While I was looking after him, I studied a great deal about nursing, and it gave me a real feeling of satisfaction. In fact I discovered a kind of vocation.

Ian came to London from time to time to visit his son, but our marriage was essentially over and on one of his visits he revealed that he had a girl friend whom he wanted to marry. It was now 1937 and the clouds of war were gathering in Europe. Hitler had come to power and was re-arming Germany contrary to the terms of the Versailles Treaty. Mr. Chamberlain's government was pretending that there was no need to worry, and that Hitler was merely rebuilding the shattered German economy and its people's self-esteem. In 1938, German troops invaded Czecho-Slovakia, a country England had pledged to defend, and so we expected war. This was when Mr. Chamberlain went to Munich to meet Hitler and returned with his infamous piece of paper, signed by Hitler, promising peace in our time. Some believed it, many did not. Against this background, Ian insisted on a divorce so that he could

## The Georgian Girl

marry Phyllis.

Nicky was at Kindergarten at the Froebel Institute on Talgarth Road. I had become friends with the parents of his school chum Gordon. Ralph, Gordon's father, was a larger than life Scotsman with a never-ending stream of jokes. Gordon's mother, Florence, was a rather dour woman from Lancashire. It was she who came to lend me support at the divorce proceedings. Afterwards we stopped for a drink to help me get over the trauma, but Florence entered into the melancholy spirit with great gusto and many drinks later it was I who had to help her back home. Florence told me she was laying in a supply of butter (probably about five pounds) which she would keep in the fridge, because Gordon loved his chips and couldn't possibly eat them if they were not fried in real butter. How anyone could imagine that the war would be over in a few weeks defied belief, but it seemed to be a widely held view at the time. Once again my thoughts turned to those young officers in Vladivostok, and I wondered what had become of them. I supposed they would be caught up in the war.

The Froebel School, like many in London, decided to evacuate to a large house in Gloucestershire. It was believed that the German air force could reach the east coast to bomb London, but that they would never get to the west of England. (No-one then imagined that France would fall). I was asked to go with the school as matron, and since this would enable me to be there with Nicky, and the school agreed to provide accommodation for my mother as well, I decided to accept their offer. However, it was quite an upheaval and travelling to Gloucester was not easy. Trains were being requisitioned by the military for the newly conscripted troops who were being sent to the country for training, and it was difficult to get a ticket. Nonetheless we all managed to get there in time for the Autumn term of 1938.

# The Georgian Girl

*Vice Admiral Alan Scott-Moncrieff on duty during WW2*

# CHAPTER 10

## WORLD WAR II AND THE BLITZ   1939-1941

After Mr. Chamberlain's return from Munich, a lot of the parents decided that the crisis was over and that it was safe to return to London, so by early 1939 the school gave up its evacuation project, and I was left without a job and with nowhere for us to live, since I had given up the flat at 104 West Kensington Court.

On the 3rd September 1939 Germany invaded Poland, so France and England declared war on Germany. I remember that day vividly. We were staying with my sister-in-law Enid, now married to Michael Corbet-Singleton, and their two children, at Dean Hall in Gloucestershire. I had come to a turning point. I didn't know whether Nicky should stay in England or not. Many parents were sending their children to America and Canada and I knew I could send Nicky to stay with my sister Lily who was living in Pennsylvania. But since I was not able to go myself, due to visa problems, I could not bear the thought of parting with him. I agonized over this decision for many days and when I could stand it no more went into Gloucester and spent the afternoon buying a hat. As I left the shop with my new purchase, I saw the headlines in the evening paper saying that a passenger liner carrying hundreds of English children had been torpedoed in mid-Atlantic and that there were no survivors, and I realized my instincts were right: somehow I had made the right decision by making no decision. But I knew that we had imposed on my sister-in-law for long enough and that I must find a job and a home.

A few days later to my great delight I heard from Alan Scott-Moncrieff, who said he had been trying to find me since learning of my divorce. He was still in the Royal Navy and was in command of HMS Enchantress based at Devonport. He told me that there were lots of employment opportunities around the naval base which was out of range of the German bombers. It seemed an attractive idea and would enable me to help the war effort - I found a suitable house in the Mutley Plain area of Plymouth and moved in during the Spring of 1940, while Nicky started at the Junior School of Plymouth College. Alan invited us both to tea in his stateroom on HMS

## The Georgian Girl

Enchantress and we were piped aboard in great ceremony.

Then the Vichy government took over in France and agreed a peace treaty with Germany. The British Expeditionary Force, which had been sent to help the French defend themselves against the German army, was forced to retreat north and was finally trapped at Dunkirk, from where they were rescued by thousands of tiny boats whose owners courageously sailed over the channel in defiance of Germany. But now that the Germans had taken France, Plymouth was easily within range of the Luftwaffe, the German Air Force, and became one of its main targets. People were building air raid shelters in their gardens, and I felt this to be a necessary precaution. Most of the shelters were rather flimsy affairs made of corrugated iron, known as Morrison Shelters, named after the Home Secretary Herbert Morrison. They were cold and damp and to my mind, not at all what was needed. Having been through a bombardment before, I instinctively felt that a secure place to live was required so using all my remaining savings, I designed and had built a reasonably comfortable shelter dug into the back garden, properly insulated, with electric lights and heat and three built-in bunk beds. It was completed in record time and not a minute too soon.

As the air raids started, we fell into the routine of listening to Lord Haw Haw (William Joyce, the Irish American, who broadcast German propaganda in the early years of the war), before cooking an evening meal in the house, then as darkness fell, taking it to the shelter to eat in safety. We then spent the evening knitting or playing cards until it was time for bed. Usually the raids would start as soon as darkness fell, and sometimes there were five or six raids in a night so there was no point in returning to the house. Neighbours would frequently drop in, including those who had scoffed at me for wasting my money on our shelter. Generally they were good company and helped to pass the time, but sometimes they overstayed their welcome as I was often quite ready to go to bed long before they left.

During the blitz everyone emulated Winston Churchill and wore a siren suit to bed. This was a one-piece woolly trouser and top which allowed one to spring from a warm bed to deal with whatever emergency might occur, such as fighting a fire or investigating anything suspicious. Only in broad daylight could one risk changing into something more formal, and taking a bath was a precarious adventure at any time.

My mother, who had not been granted British nationality and was therefore considered a stateless person and an alien, had to register at the local police station every month. She was forbidden to ride a bicycle in case she acted as a courier of state secrets. The idea of my frail, elderly mother acting as a spy and riding a

## The Georgian Girl

bicycle, (something she had never done) was ludicrous, but rules were rules. I did however put my foot down when the local policeman spotted Nicky's new bike and wanted to confiscate it, but in the end he saw the funny side and relented.

Ian rang me one day to announce that he wanted to bring his new wife Phyllis to stay in Plymouth for a week to visit his son. Although I thought it strange, obviously I could not object, so I made the arrangements for them to stay in a house up the road where there were rooms to let. When they arrived, I invited them to spend the evening with us. Not unexpectedly, there was a bad air raid. A firebomb fell about three houses away, and as a dutiful neighbour I rushed out with the stirrup pump and a bucket of water to help put out the fire. Ian came with me and carried the bucket of water; Phyllis, clearly terrified, volunteered to stay in the shelter and look after Nicky and my mother. It was a poignant moment as Ian and I stood side by side to fight the fire. Next morning Ian and Phyllis packed up and left.

One morning, after a particularly eventful night, I took Nicky to school as usual. As we rounded the final bend, what was left of the school came into view. It was a pile of rubble. This is of course the stuff of every schoolchild's fondest dream and Nicky was no exception. He was jumping up and down amid hoots of joy, and from then on I did my best to educate him at home.

The raids went on almost every night through the winter and into the spring of 1941. Early in March I decided to have a blitz of my own on the garden. Nicky worked with me, and we planted a lot of flowers, cut the grass front and back, and spent the entire day raking, tidying up, and throwing away rubbish. As dusk fell, the garden really looked lovely. That very evening the bomb fell. We had finished dinner in the shelter, cleared away the plates, and were settling down to a game of lotto (bingo), when the raids started. There were continuing waves of bombers, and bombs falling all around. I believe this was part of the final push by the Luftwaffe to break our spirit. Suddenly there was the most tremendous bang accompanied by a cold wind coming through the door, which had been closed but now lay broken on the floor, and Bill the cat arrived on my lap just as the lights went out. The darkness was followed by the sound of breaking glass, splintering wood, and of tiles sliding off the roof and smashing on the ground, and then, just as suddenly, an eerie silence. For a moment I thought I was being propelled through the cold air and would soon be landing against something hard and that would be my end. Then I called out and found that Nicky and my mother were still in the shelter with me and that we were all alive, as well as Bill. We lit candles and bedded down for the rest of the night in very cold and draughty surroundings.

Next morning we found that the house was a roofless shell. Part of the second floor had collapsed, and my bed was now in the living room. I cannot describe the mess in the garden – masonry and broken glass lay everywhere – it was all a disaster area. Mother and I were able to retrieve two suitcases into which we packed essential clothing, and I managed to find a working telephone and called a taxi, and soon we were on our way back to Dean Hall.

It was very peaceful in Gloucestershire, and a huge contrast to the nightly dangers of living through the blitz. Sometimes at night we could hear the throbbing of German aeroplanes on their way to bomb the industrial midlands. To me, they seemed to be saying, "Going to Birmingham….Going to Birmingham…." but at least they were not bombing us.

A few days after we had settled into rooms at Dean Hall, I decided something had to be done with our furniture and belongings in Plymouth, so I telephoned and asked Pickfords the removers to collect anything still in one piece from the house. "Where can we pick up the key?" was their first question. I began to laugh hysterically; "There is no front door," I explained when I had got a grip on myself, "In fact there are no doors standing any longer." They agreed to do what they could. Eventually what was left of the furniture arrived in Gloucestershire, and went into storage.

Now I had to make some plans for the future. Two things were pressing; we needed somewhere of our own to live, and I badly needed a job, as we had very little money. My sister-in-law Enid had very kindly said that we were welcome to live at Dean Hall for as long as we liked, but I wanted a house of my own. Houses in the country away from the bombing were almost impossible to find, but she knew of a derelict cottage nearby, which belonged to a neighbour, a Mrs. Jacques, who said we could move in if we could make it habitable. Mill Cottage had been an old cider mill - the original millstone was still in place - and it was situated near the crest of the hill known as Pleasant Stile, with beautiful views of the Severn Valley and the village of Westbury-on-Severn. There were two rooms downstairs and a scullery, and three tiny bedrooms upstairs. There was no gas or electricity, no bathroom, and no running water. Just outside the front door there was a well with a bucket, and some distance away at the back of the cottage was an outside privy.

During the war it was extremely difficult to get building work done. Most skilled men had joined up, and anyone left behind was needed for priority work. I had a job to convince the authorities that work on Mill Cottage was a priority, but somehow I succeeded. Electricity was brought to the house, power points provided to each of the rooms, and mains water was provided by means of a single tap over the sink in the kitchen. As to toilet facilities, I ordered a chemical lavatory, known as an Alsan, which was installed at the back of the scullery, as far as possible from the main

## The Georgian Girl

house, but thankfully indoors. It contained a black liquid disinfectant, which had a very strong smell, something like creosote. Rather than wait for a decorator, I bought rolls of wallpaper and papered each of the rooms myself before ordering the delivery of our remaining furniture. Mrs. Jacques arranged to have the outside painted, but to my horror, when the decorator came he painted it bright orange, which would not have been my choice, but which was probably the only paint available. It could be seen from miles away, and I thought it would become a landmark for every German bomber that wanted to dump its last bombs on England before going home. As it turned out, the colour mellowed quite quickly and we were not bombed.

Meanwhile, I found a job in a local factory in Mitcheldean, about four miles away, run by a Mr. Tomes, who lived in the garden flat at Dean Hall. He had a terrific American sports car called a Terraplane, which he used to drive to his factory everyday and sometimes I got a lift with him. All able-bodied women in England were required to work to help the war effort and of course, I desperately needed the money. I had never seen the inside of a factory before, so it was quite a challenging experience. I'm not sure what it was we were making, but I believe it was some vital parts for Spitfires. It was all cloaked in great secrecy. My job was to hand out the tools, and I had to learn quickly about taps and dies and the various sizes of drills and so forth.

Enid's husband Michael, who had been a rubber-planter in Malaya before the war, and had lost everything when the Japanese invaded, had planted an apple orchard of seven acres at Dean Hall, which was their means of support. It was hard work; he had to be up at dawn every day to keep up the grounds and spray the apples and eventually pick and pack them for the market. He had one man, Francis Brain, who understood how to grow apples and worked extremely hard to make it a success, and Michael's son John also helped when he was not away at school. At weekends, Michael captained the local Home Guard, and could be seen marching his troops up and down the drive, at first carrying broomsticks and later rifles.

Enid somehow managed to sell the apples, which meant she had a lot of deliveries to make all over the county. Her car was a rather ancient Vauxhall for which she had a petrol allowance, as her job of distributing food was considered essential. It had a dicky seat in which her daughter Gillie and Nicky used to ride. It was a miracle they didn't fall out and just as well that I was busy at the factory and didn't know about it until much later.

So we settled down to a routine. I worked part-time at Mr. Tomes's factory, and Nicky went by bicycle to his school at Flaxley Abbey on Monday mornings and returned on Friday afternoons. Mother did most of the cooking on a coalburning

## The Georgian Girl

stove and together we planted vegetables in the garden and tried to be as self-supporting as possible. Bathing was a problem - someone lent us a hipbath, but I found it easier to wash myself in parts. The bath was used once a week on Friday evenings for Nicky. The procedure was to place it in front of the kitchen stove and then use every kettle, pot and pan in the house to heat the water and empty it into the bath.

Apart from these inconveniences, we were all very happy at Mill Cottage and even Bill seemed content. Nicky had his bicycle and used it to visit nearby towns and villages and to go to Dean Hall to see his cousins. There was a local shop at Pleasant Stile, just across the road, useful for newspapers and sweets. The garden was a delight; every kind of fruit tree was there, including Victoria plums and many varieties of apples. We also had raspberries, gooseberries, and a large strawberry patch. As a dutiful supporter of "Digging for Victory", I planted rows of lettuces, beans, peas, cabbages, tomatoes, and potatoes, making us almost self-supporting in food.

After a couple of years of this pleasant, but uninspiring existence, I felt I could no longer stand the isolation, and must return to a city and a more urban life. The Battle of Britain had been won, the RAF had control of the skies over England, and the bombing had stopped. Life in London appeared to be quite safe, so I decided to return there to live.

# CHAPTER 11

## LONDON DURING THE WAR YEARS AND AFTER 1942-1950

My old friend Arthur Hodges was living in a tiny flat in Chelsea Cloisters on Sloane Avenue. By then he was almost eighty years old, but still a robust figure with a zest for life. He told me he had tried to do his bit during the Battle of Britain by volunteering to be a fire warden. He stated his age as sixty-four (the maximum allowed), but when he was asked to climb a very flimsy ladder to the roof some sixty feet above the ground, he had not been able to do it and had had to admit to being seventy-seven.

Arthur suggested I contact the American Red Cross, which was running hostels for American servicemen on leave in London. As it happened, they were desperately in need of help, and after a very short training in first aid I was hired as a receptionist at the Hans Crescent Club, a rather smart hotel before the war, and after it a Magistrates Court. At the same time I was able to rent a flat in West Kensington Court where we had lived before the war, this time number 121 on the fifth floor. Mother and I moved back to London and I arranged for Nicky to go to a prep school at Shackleford in Surrey, which seemed sufficiently far from London to avoid any potential resurgence of bombing.

The servicemen's club in Hans Crescent was quite fun. Quickly it was nicknamed the Hans Christian Club by the Yanks. These young men were mostly eighteen or nineteen years old, away from home for the first time. They all chewed gum and ate candy which they couldn't resist feeding to a pet monkey that lived there. The poor monkey, I regret to say, came to a sticky end. We asked the men not to feed it, but they were like children, keen to find new friends, even if only with a monkey. Mostly they were the crews of the B17 Flying Fortresses making nightly bombing raids on Germany. We would sometimes see them two or three times during a few weeks and then no more. No doubt some were transferred to other duties, but quite a number were shot down. It was very sad when they just disappeared for one reason

## The Georgian Girl

or another, particularly for some of the girls working with me who had gone out with them. But life was like that during the war - everything was transitory.

Then quite unexpectedly I was approached by a man from Military Intelligence and offered a job as a temporary civil servant. Clearly I was recruited for my language skills, and assigned to the French desk in Bush House. The work had two parts; monitoring broadcasts and censoring letters. It was not only fascinating but also vital, and of great value to the war effort. Among the letters I read were some exchanged between General de Gaulle and his wife, and I was asked to comment on what might be his real agenda. My opinion was that even then he aspired to become the leader of France after the war. I remember Pauline, one of my assistants, repeatedly saying in a loud voice, "Oh, Mrs. Mac! There you are surrounded by all your French letters." A French letter was at that time a colloquial term for a condom - after a while it became a rather tired joke.

While I was doing this work, a call came round for French-speaking volunteers to meet some of the Free French servicemen stationed in England. I was put in touch with two sailors, Misha and Leon, who served on a submarine and I saw them whenever they were on leave. Misha was the younger man, Leon a more senior officer.

Now London experienced a new peril, Hitler's secret weapon, the V-1 rocket known as a doodlebug, which was a bomb attached to a fairly basic ramjet engine. It was kept straight by a gyroscope, and loaded with just sufficient fuel to get it to its target. Doodlebugs travelled a bit faster than Spitfires, and dropped their bombs without warning at all hours of the night and day. One of the first missed London by about thirty miles and landed quite close to Nicky's school. I happened to visit him on the following Sunday, getting to Godalming by train and walking the last two miles. When I got there the headmaster, Mr. Hill, took the parents aside and told us about the doodlebug, and said that the boys had not been told anything, and for reasons of national security we should keep silent on this matter. Duly warned, I started to walk with Nicky out of the school to one of the local tearooms. As we left the grounds, he proudly produced from his pocket a strange looking metallic object, and announced that it was a piece of the doodlebug. So much for national security!

The doodlebugs were particularly menacing and unpleasant. We heard them approaching, sounding rather like a loud motorcycle. Suddenly the noise stopped; then we all dived for cover as it meant the thing was coming down and would explode on impact. Appalling damage often ensued, and we learned of one that landed in a crowded restaurant at Troy Court where at least a hundred diners were killed. At first there was no defence against them. Barrage balloons, very effective

## The Georgian Girl

against low flying aircraft and dive-bombers, were of no help, and there was no aircraft capable of matching their speed. Eventually some of the fighter pilots, at great personal risk, developed a technique of flying into the path of the doodlebug, allowing it to pass close to one side and as it flew by, tipping it over by wing contact. Occasionally, it was possible to return the bomb back to where it came from, which of course was tremendously satisfactory, although I doubt if any of them flew further than into the Channel.

Ultimately, Werner Von Braun's V-2 rockets were to come. These were the first missiles to travel beyond the earth's atmosphere and they were deadly. There was no warning of their arrival, and no defence whatsoever. Luckily the problem of re-entry into the atmosphere had not been fully resolved, and many burned up. Just in time the D-Day invasion was mounted on 6th June 1944, and not long after that the V-2 base at Peenemunde was captured. If this rocket development had been allowed to continue, the damage to England would have been immense.

Although relatively few V-2 rockets succeeded, the barrage of doodlebugs continued with devastating effect. One day I got a call from Leon to say that Misha had been sheltering from an air raid, and had just given up his safe place to a young woman when a doodlebug fell. Misha was severely injured, and was rushed to hospital. Of course I went to visit him, but he died soon after. I never saw Leon again. I have often wondered what became of him.

The last years of the war were a very busy, satisfying part of my life as I felt I was doing something useful. I saw my beloved Alan from time to time and we would go out to dinner or to the theatre together (theatre performances had continued during the bombing.) Once in a while Misha and Leon came for dinner giving me the opportunity to practise my spoken French. Also I had befriended a Russian-American while working at the Hans Crescent Club, and as he spoke a bit of Russian, my mother and I were also able to keep up our skills in that language. His name was Stiopa and he had decided to become a Russian Orthodox priest when he returned to his home in Ohio. He survived the war and wrote to me on his return, but I don't know whether he went into the priesthood.

By now the war was going our way, and each day at work we studied the Allied advances on the map. The Russians were advancing at a tremendous rate and the race to reach Berlin was in full swing. Then suddenly (it seemed) it was all over and on 8th May 1945, we celebrated Victory in Europe. Nicky had just started school at Charterhouse. My nephew Greg, who was in the US Fleet Air Arm, was stationed in Paris on his last assignment, taking care of the Soviet aircrews who were ferrying the last of the Lend-Lease aircraft to Russia. Greg decided to write himself some

## The Georgian Girl

orders to fly to England to visit me, and as he was also quite keen to see Nicky, I rang up Robert Birley, the headmaster at Charterhouse, to see if we could visit him. As an Allied naval officer, Greg was immediately invited to lunch at the top table. The two of us took the train to Godalming, but what we did not know was that there had also been VE Day celebrations at Charterhouse. After all the boys were supposedly tucked up in bed for the night, Nicky and some of his chums had broken out of their house and walked down to Godalming to continue celebrations on their own. Unfortunately, on the way out, the school Sergeant had noticed them and given chase. In the dark, Nicky had run straight into the low-hanging branch of a tree, and although able to continue with the adventure, awoke the following morning sporting two very black eyes. When we arrived, he was summoned to the headmaster's study and as he appeared, we were all stunned at his appearance. Greg was the first to recover and said, "I'd hate to see what the other guy looks like." Robert Birley tried to pass it off as an everyday occurrence, but Greg's comment made the rounds, and Nicky acquired a new nickname of Killer among the boys.

At the end of the war, my civil service career ended. I was desperate for any kind of employment. Pauline, my colleague in the French section, had heard that a new theatre was being opened in the East End of London to be called The People's Palace and that they were looking for a wardrobe mistress. Knowing that I made most of my own clothes, she suggested I apply. In the event I was taken on by the theatre in the Mile End Road and made and fitted clothes on some of the leading actors and actresses of the day including John Mills, who became a friend and many others. It was great fun and a new world for me, but not one in which I wanted to make a permanent career.

Luckily, just as the first production, The Beggars Opera, was completed, I was asked if I would like to help in a programme of re-education of German prisoners-of-war, still in camps throughout Britain. I was to travel to these camps all over the country, and organized a series of lectures on the democratic system of government. Of course I accepted and I was delighted to be involved once more in work of national importance. One of the lecturers turned out to be Robert Birley. Some of the camps were as far afield as Scotland, and to get there I took my first ever flight in a very dilapidated Dakota (DC3) aircraft.

My mother also made her first journey by air at about the same time. She had now been living with me for almost ten years, including all the difficult war years, and she was becoming rather a worry as her memory was starting to fail. I felt that she should not be left on her own while I was doing this work, and after corresponding with my sister Lily, she agreed that mother should live with her in Pennsylvania. So

## The Georgian Girl

after tearful farewells mother boarded a Pan American Clipper to the United States in late 1947. To make such a journey then was quite an adventure, as crossing the Atlantic non-stop was beyond the limit of most aircraft, and I believe this one had to stop in Iceland to refuel.

At that time England seemed a very bleak and uninspiring place. When the war had been over for more than two years, there were still shortages of everything, which seemed to be getting even more severe. For the first time, even bread was rationed. Prices of all goods were now rising, but wages were not, and the returning servicemen were having difficulty finding jobs. It appeared to be a replay of 1919. Although an American loan had been accepted by Mr. Atlee's government, it was not being used to rebuild the country's industrial base as it was in other European countries, which was what America originally had intended. Instead, it was used to change the political landscape of Britain by nationalizing its industries, bringing the economy into public ownership. Against this backdrop Nicky, now seventeen, was completing his education at Charterhouse and wondering what his next step should be. He expressed some interest in going to university, but his father, who had by then fulfilled his legal obligation of support, did not intend to offer any help in this respect.

After much soul-searching Nicky decided to try to get closer to his father to enlist his support for university. Because some of his friends had successfully hitch-hiked throughout Britain, he suggested to Ian the two of them hitch-hike together to Wales for a week, staying at various bed and breakfasts along the way. I don't know how well it went, but on his return, Nicky told me that Ian had refused point-blank to support him through university. Nicky had then said, "Right, I'm off to America to work my way, as I understand it can be done in the U.S.A." I must say that I was horrified at the idea of losing him, but felt that I must support him if that was what he wanted to do, so with a heavy heart I put into motion the necessary arrangements. Nicky was quickly granted a visa and booked on a freighter leaving from the Port of London in November 1948. Meanwhile my sister agreed he could stay with her at least to begin with.

At the same time, I made enquiries as to how I could go too. American immigration policy was then based on the country of origin, the object being to retain the ethnic composition of the United States as it had been originally established. This meant that anyone born in England was processed at once, but for people born in other countries, the delay could be considerable. This was the same problem I had encountered in 1941. Because I had been born in Georgia – which was part of Russia – and the Cold War between America and the USSR had begun, the American authorities labelled

## The Georgian Girl

me a Soviet citizen, and refused me a visa. I remonstrated vigorously, and pointed out that the Soviet regime had not existed when I was born, and that I had never lived in the Soviet Republic, but it was to no avail. It was two years before I was finally granted a visa for travel to the United States, and only then was I able arrange my passage to New York. After that there followed a mad scramble to dispose of my flat and my furniture, and make final visits to all my English friends. I describe these now as *final* visits to my friends, because then a journey across the Atlantic was a rare occurrence - sailing to America took six days on the fastest ships and cost more money than most people earned in six months.

I sailed on the Queen Elizabeth in 1950, not expecting to return to England for a long time, and believing the United States would be my home for the rest of my life.

# CHAPTER 12

## THE UNITED STATES   1950-1954

I love travelling by ship. Everything about it appeals to me. I enjoy the ship's motion, and the clean sea air, but even more, I love the bustle of the sailors, and the excellent food and good company at mealtimes, particularly if one is invited to sit at the Captain's table, as I was. When we arrived and sailed past the Statue of Liberty, I felt the same emotional stir that I had had when I arrived for the first time in 1922.

My nephew, Gregory Gagarin, with his young bride Ann, met me as soon as I had cleared Immigration and Customs and they drove me to State College, the town in Pennsylvania where Lily and Gushka and my mother lived. Mother seemed to have aged considerably in the three years since I had last seen her, but I was glad to see her. I was given a warm welcome and a wonderful dinner and was re-united with Nicky, by then a nineteen-year-old university student, looking well, but somewhat undernourished

My initial reaction to State College was one of mild shock. I was amazed at the laid back informality of this university town - I suppose I had been expecting something more like Oxford. The local people were friendly, but completely unaware of the wider world. The war, which had been such an overwhelmingly important part of my life, and which had shaped my views and opinions on many things, seemed not to have touched this pleasant, rural part of America. Coming from Europe, I knew that America's entry into the war had helped to change its course in our favour, and I had therefore assumed that the country which had sent so many thousands of its sons to fight and die in Europe and the Far East must have been deeply affected. But here in Pennsylvania and, I later realized most of America, people were barely aware that there had been a world war. I remember remarks made to me quite casually such as, "We had rationing here too. One day each week, we had to go without meat," and, "So-and-So's son in the next town was a prisoner of war in Japan." Popular feeling was that the war was over, America had a new president, the war hero General Eisenhower, and that now people were more interested in the future, and in making money as fast as possible because they believed the terrible economic depression which had continued right up to the war would return. In sharp contrast to war-ravaged England, America was a land of abundance - so many enormous cars, so many goods of all kinds in the shops, so much money in people's pockets - even Nicky, who had a humble part-time job in one of the university offices, was planning to buy his first car.

The big question now for me was how to support myself. My wartime experiences and language skills were of no interest to the university, the only employer of any size in State College. Gushka, who had a teaching post, did his best to find work for me, and eventually I was offered a job preparing punched cards for the new computer that had just been installed in the administration department. It was very boring, but it provided me with a living, and enabled me to pay my sister something for continuing to provide a home for me. After a while I found a small two-bedroom house nearby and Nicky agreed to share it with me, so I began to feel more optimistic, but alas, it was not to last. In 1951 President Eisenhower had decided to resist any further communist expansion in Asia and the Korean War began. Nicky was eligible to be drafted into military service, and he joined the Pennsylvania Air National Guard. Although he continued with his courses, he expected to be called to active duty at any time.

Meanwhile my poor mother, who by that time was becoming more forgetful, often complained that she was unhappy living with my sister. I suppose I should have taken her in, but the house was too small for three of us and I felt I could not cope. After much discussion and heart-searching, Lily and I decided to put mother in an old people's home on Long Island run by some Russians. We hoped that she would find some kindred spirits there, and could live out her life in some kind of tranquility. I felt dreadful for abandoning her, and went to visit her as often as I could, but she was not happy. She died a few years later, and after the funeral my thoughts and feelings for her were of great sadness.

This was not a happy time in my life. The job was tedious and dispiriting, I felt terribly alien in this small Pennsylvania town, and I longed for the stimulation and sophistication that one finds in a major city, so one week-end I went to visit my old friend Julie Hodges. She was then living in New York, apparently totally involved with doing good works, and in particular providing aid to poor Greek orphans through the World Church Service, which was based in New York. Julie's appearance was not at all sophisticated, and I was rather shocked by the sloppy kind of clothes she chose to wear, for she was very wealthy, and could have afforded much better ones. In fact on a visit to an estate agent, where she expressed an interest in renting a flat in Greenwich Village, the agent foolishly said that he didn't

## The Georgian Girl

think she could afford it. Nicky told me that when he had first arrived in America he had visited Julie's mother Polly who was living alone in New England. On the walls of her house there were several old master paintings. Polly Hodges never cooked, she told Nicky, because the fumes from the stove might spoil the Rembrandts

Julie and I had a wonderful weekend and she promised she would ask the Church World Service if it could find a job for me. You can imagine my surprise when a few days after returning to State College, she called me to ask me to return to New York for an interview. As a result I was offered a job, starting immediately, in which I would be travelling mostly by air all over the United States, co-ordinating the organization's charitable endeavours and fundraising activities. The pay was barely adequate, but the nature of the work so much more rewarding than what I had been doing in State College.

At that time I also made contact with an old childhood friend from Russia, Tatiana Schvetzoff. She was living in a large apartment on Central Park West, and sharing it with some of the troupe of the Ballet Russe de Monte Carlo, including her nephew Igor Shvetzoff and his two dogs, Grande and Piccolo. Grande was a huge Russian wolfhound, Piccolo a Pekinese, and when Igor, a strikingly beautiful man, took them for a walk in Central Park, the three of them were quite a sight. I moved in to Tatiana's apartment, joining the bohemian, artistic circle of lodgers from ballet dancers to film actors and playwrights.

Then the job petered out, and The World Church Service gave me two weeks notice. So I was now obliged once more to do a lot of soul-searching to decide how best to support myself and help Nicky financially. A woman in my mid-fifties, I had no qualifications, and I knew I must get some training if I wanted a job that would stand me in good stead for the rest of my life. Tatiana had been a nurse before she had retired, and had found it very rewarding. I decided to follow her suggestion, and qualify as a Practical Nurse. Thinking back to when I had taken a First Aid course in London during the Blitz, I remembered it had been interesting, and that I had had a natural aptitude for it. To do the training, I first had to take a High School Diploma which I learnt I could do by correspondence, and could then enroll at Bethel Hospital in New York.

I loved the training and I got on well with the other nurses. Once I had qualified, I stayed on at Bethel Hospital for a while, but at my age I began to find the physical nature of hospital work too heavy, and I decided to register with an agency as a private nurse, which was both less tiring and financially much more rewarding. Many of my patients became good friends, but I had one or two unnerving experiences. Once, as I was cleaning up the kitchen after preparing a meal, I opened the door

## The Georgian Girl

beneath the kitchen sink, expecting to find a bin. Instead, I was confronted by a large black snake. For a moment we looked each other in the eye, then I very gently closed the door, and went to inform my patient that there was a snake in her kitchen. "That is Henry," she said immediately. "I should have told you about him. I hope you didn't frighten him." Needless to say, I left that job immediately.

# CHAPTER 13

## LIFE IN CALIFORNIA AND TO NEW YORK AGAIN 1954-1957

By the beginning of 1954, Nicky had completed his final year at Penn State University and had taken a degree in Electrical Engineering. Now he wanted to go to California, and we agreed to drive there together. He bought a rather old convertible car, and in February we set off in deep snow. I had not got a valid driving licence, but I did have a New York learner's permit, so I was able to share some of the driving. It was a fascinating journey; the long straight stretches of road across the prairies were dotted with small mid-western towns, each with its own Main Street where one found the same branded gas-station, diner, and Sears Roebuck store. When we reached Texas, the landscape became even more extensive, and half a dozen cowboys rode by. It was the first time I had ever seen real working cowboys, and it gave me a big thrill. I must say I felt a certain fascination for Texas, a place where they say the men are men and the women are damn glad of it.

We continued through the cactus-strewn desert into California and the Imperial Valley, where it was very hot, even in February. We finally reached Los Angeles in the early afternoon. Our first impression was that it was a city dominated by freeways and traffic, and that the boulevards were lined with that style of palm tree that has a long trunk and a clump of foliage at the top. While observing these rather strange looking trees, one of them suddenly burst into flames. A few minutes later two fire engines rushed up with sirens blazing, and put out the fire. We did not discover why the tree ignited, but it was quite an introduction to Los Angeles. We stayed there only one day. On the whole, I didn't think much of it. It seemed to have little character and although it was marvellous to drive in an open car in early February, with the warm weather also came the most unpleasant smell of fumes, the famous Los Angeles smog. The following day we drove north on the beautiful Pacific Coast highway, stopping briefly at Malibu, Santa Barbara, and Pismo Beach. Since Pismo is the Russian word for a letter (of the kind you receive in the post), I decided we must stop there for the night. No Russians were to be seen, but we later learned that when Alaska was part of Russia, many of them had explored the west coast of America as far south as Pismo and maybe further.

The next day we drove on to Monterey and Carmel. In Monterey, we stopped for lunch on Cannery Row of Steinbeck fame - the sardine canneries were still very active then. We found a café for our lunch where abalone was the dish of day and it was absolutely delicious. In 1954, tourists were just beginning to visit Monterey Peninsula.

We continued up the coast the next day through some of the most spectacular scenery I had ever seen, arriving at last in San Francisco in the late afternoon. Not having any idea where to go, and having only a rudimentary tourist map, we made for the area of greatest activity, and found ourselves at the main Post Office on 7$^{th}$ Street. After finding a place to leave the car, we looked for a reasonable hotel to spend a night or two, and eventually checked in at the Roosevelt. Further exploration brought us to a little restaurant where we celebrated our arrival with a meal and a glass of Californian wine. After that we strolled to Union Square which was full of elegant shops such as I. Magnin and Bullocks. I thought San Francisco was a beautiful city, built as it was on seven hills and surrounded on three sides by water. I loved the sounds of the cable cars and of the traffic lights which clanked as two metal plates, red and green, were raised or lowered, reminding me of old railway signals.

The next morning Nicky telephoned Stanford University and arranged an appointment for the following day. I rang a friend of my sister living in Palo Alto, who told me she would be delighted to put us up for a few nights. The following day, a Wednesday, we drove south down the peninsula on the El Camino Real into what is now known as Silicon Valley. In those days the area was still countrified, and Burlingame, San Mateo, and Menlo Park were market towns selling agricultural produce grown in the valley. Arriving in Palo Alto in time for lunch at a local sandwich shop, we then made our way to Stanford University. The main approach was along Palm Drive, and a fleeting hope that we might stop and picnic off dates from the trees was quickly dashed when we realised they were not date palms. Palm Drive leads to a circular road and the university stands beyond, an impressive set of sandstone buildings and cloisters centred on the chapel. To the left and behind the main buildings stands the Hoover Tower, the building housing the Hoover Presidential Library, and to the right is a complex of buildings of the School of Engineering. We found the Dean's office and while Nicky had his interview, I walked round the campus. It was very different from any other university I had seen, and

## The Georgian Girl

quite unlike Oxford or Cambridge or even Penn State. I think the difference was its informality, perhaps because of a more modern approach to learning.

We stayed two days in Palo Alto, before returning to Los Angeles for more interviews. This second visit confirmed my initial impression that I did not Like Los Angeles. It seemed to me brash and phony, a city without a centre and a place where people lived in their cars. Even meals were taken at drive-in restaurants, a common event nowadays, but a new concept in the 1950s. As soon as we could, we returned to San Francisco and fortunately Nicky was offered a place at Stanford starting immediately. We managed to find him a tiny apartment close to the university and I made plans to return to New York to resume my nursing career since I was now down to my last dollar. Tatiana very kindly gave me the room in her flat once more and refused any payment until I was earning again.

I had been in the United States for five years by now, and was eligible to apply for citizenship. Remembering the difficulty I had had in being allowed entry and the insult of being classified a Soviet Citizen, I applied immediately, and after taking the required citizenship course, I was sworn in.

This was really the start of the next phase of my life, when I started seriously to think of my future. I had no assets except my nursing qualification and no pension, and I was fast approaching sixty. It looked as if I would spend the remainder of my life in the United States, and I was determined to save some of my earnings and to make sure I worked the necessary ten years to qualify for U.S. Social Security. I was particularly concerned that I would not become a burden on anyone in my old age, and so I plunged into the world of private nursing. I met a wide variety of patients, some of whom were ghastly, though many others became friends, but for the first time in my life I was able to put some money aside.

I worked extremely hard for more than a year. Tatiana was a good friend, and we had some very enjoyable times with the wide variety of people who dropped in for a meal or a bed for the night or just to talk. Tennessee Williams was an occasional visitor – he seemed quiet and self-contained to me. Marlon Brando also came from time to time, but as I was working very hard I did not meet him - as anyone can imagine, I much regret it.

Nonetheless, I missed Nicky, and although we often spoke on the telephone, I longed to see him and decided that I must live closer. My nursing licence was valid only in New York State, and I realized I would have to take another exam to be able to work in California, which meant going to live there. Tatiana suggested asking the Bethel Hospital, where I had trained, if they could help, and after much discussion I was put in touch with Mills Hospital in San Mateo, California, where I was offered

## The Georgian Girl

employment and a place in the nurses' home. I set off in February on a Greyhound bus, on what would have been an uneventful journey but for the very severe winter. The snow in Colorado and Utah made some of the roads almost impassable, and on the famous Route 66, near Salt Lake City, the bus gracefully slithered off the road into a ditch. No one was hurt, but we were trapped in the bus until the Utah Highway Patrol arrived. A most handsome young officer carried me to safety, and after a short time we were driven into Salt Lake City, and given shelter and hot coffee until another bus arrived to take us on to San Francisco.

My time at Mills Hospital was pleasant enough, but the pay was very little and life in a nurses' home rather restricting. San Mateo was then a rather sleepy small town with a good array of shops and a few nice restaurants. Nicky and I used to have dinner together about once a week, often at Le Tricolor, which produced very nice French food at a price I could just about afford. I was very short of money, but once I had qualified as a nurse in California, I intended to take up private nursing once more. As the nurses' agency was in San Francisco, I found a tiny flat nearby.

After more than a year of working very hard, I decided it was time for a holiday in England. Nicky too was wondering whether or not to return (possibly to join the Royal Navy) and I was longing to see my old friends, especially Tony and Joan Coke, who were now living in Wiltshire. Before leaving, I wrote to Alan Scott-Moncrieff about the possibilities of a naval commission for Nicky. Then in June 1957 the two of us travelled to England on the Queen Mary. From Southampton we made our way to 53 Queen's Gate in London where I had rented a flat.

It was a wonderful summer. Nicky's American girl friend, June, came to stay for part of the time, and although he abandoned his plan to join the Navy - much to my chagrin - he had interviews with a number of British defence contractors. Sadly, the time flew and eventually I had to return to New York to earn my living. I sailed on the Queen Elizabeth in September and Igor Shvetzoff met me and took me back to Tatiana's apartment on Central Park West.

# CHAPTER 14

## BACK TO CALIFORNIA AND ON TO ENGLAND FOR A REUNION   1958-1969

In 1958, I felt that I could not stand another hot New York summer. Air conditioning was just starting to be introduced, but neither Tatiana's flat nor most of the patients' homes were fitted with it, so in May I flew back to San Francisco. I stayed with Nicky for a few days while looking for a flat, and eventually found one at 952 Sutter Street.

Nicky was working for an electronics company on the Peninsula and having a very active social life. Soon after I arrived he was offered a job in Monterey, a hundred and fifty miles away to the South and he announced he was going to marry June. The date was set for Thanksgiving Day 1958. Beforehand I gave the bridal party a breakfast at the Cliff House. It was a stormy November day and the waves were crashing onto the beach below, which was most spectacular, but not, I hoped, an omen for Nicky and June's married life. The wedding took place in a charming Episcopal Church on 7$^{th}$ Avenue and after the reception, the couple set off for their new home in Carmel, a pretty cottage surrounded by pine trees. My first grandchild, David, was born in April 1960 and I was thrilled. I visited them in Carmel as often as possible to help with the baby.

Now Nicky was on the move again, this time to Newport Beach in southern California, but then calamity fell. On July 22$^{nd}$ 1960 David died suddenly, without any warning. It was a terrible shock to us all.

Shortly after, I went to visit Nicky and June who had bought a house in the town of Costa Mesa in Orange County. During the journey I began to feel very ill indeed. I had no idea what was wrong with me, but I arrived only to stagger into bed, where I stayed for the next five days hovering at death's door. June was very kind and looked after me very well, bringing me cups of broth, which was all I could eat. The doctor also had no idea what I was suffering from - he thought I would probably die, and so did I. But after a week my strength started to return, and I was able to get up and sit in the garden in the sun, and from then on I began to recover my health. In retrospect I think I was exhausted, and my body had just packed up.

Now I had to take stock again. At the age of sixty, clearly my working days were over, and although I now had a monthly social security cheque, it was not sufficient for my support. I was sure that I could not afford to live decently in New York or San Francisco, and I did not wish to burden Nicky and June any longer. Then Nicky offered me some financial help to enable me to return to England, where the cost of living was much lower. In the spring of 1961 I moved back to London, where I stayed initially with Winn Shaw, who had been Nicky's governess some twenty-four years previously. However, it was not a very satisfactory arrangement and when my niece Gillie (Enid's daughter - she had just married a soldier, Captain Richard Rowland, and had moved into a mews house in Earls Court) asked me to come and stay with them, I was immensely grateful. It turned out to be a very happy time. We all got on well, and I think I helped them over some of the rough patches in their period of adjustment to married life. At the same time, I began to rebuild my circle of friends, all of whom were most generous and supportive. Whenever possible, I went out to Wiltshire to see Tony and Joan Coke. Then someone told me of an elderly, blind friend, who needed a live-in companion with nursing skills - would I be interested? Naturally I was interested, and I took the room adjoining Mrs. Stringer's in a South Kensington Hotel. My duties were light, and her son visited us regularly. I made a little money and had very few expenses.

Nicky and June came to England for the summer of 1962, bringing their new baby, Douglas. I found a flat for them in Redcliffe Gardens, and Douglas was christened at St. Mary the Boltons. By chance I found a flat for myself at West Kensington Court, the building where I had lived so many years, both before and during the war. I looked after Douglas, while Nicky and June decorated it for me, and then we all went furniture hunting. It was great fun and the summer passed very happily. At the end of it, Nicholas and his family returned to Washington DC where he took up a post with NASA.

I continued to look after Mrs. Stringer, and to meet old friends. Alan, by now an Admiral, was in touch and we met for lunches and trips to the theatre. But then a few years later, on a visit to the Coke's in Wiltshire, Joan gave a party at which she introduced me to Sir Reginald Savory. Perhaps I knew him, she said, since he had been part of the British military mission to Russia, and had been in Vladivostok. Little did she know that he was one of the two young captains, who had saved our lives, and got us out of Russia on the Japanese freighter in 1919. We had so much to talk about. He had made a military career in India and Burma, and he had also made a visit to the Soviet Union as a military attaché during World War II. He had married a woman rather older than himself, a widow, who had died recently. I asked him if he still had the claret jug which my mother had given him in 1919 and was delighted to learn that he had it among his most treasured possessions.

Reggie had a tiny flat in Fleet, Hampshire, and I went to have lunch with him from time to time, and he came to see me in London. We were certainly a rather ancient courting couple, but I suppose that is what we were. Eventually Reggie did the decent thing and proposed to me. I wasn't sure that I wanted to marry again - I had many reservations and I kept him waiting for quite some time, but finally I accepted. Our wedding day was 24th April 1969, and after a civil ceremony at Caxton Hall, we returned to Nicky's and June's new house at Ham Common, (Nicky was on a temporary assignment in London, with a NATO consortium) They now had three children – Douglas (seven), Suzan (five) and Robert (two). June gave us a lovely reception, and the children were excited to have a new grandfather. To add to the pleasure of the day, my nephew Greg flew into Heathrow (a noble thing to do as he was on a business trip to Belgium) and to celebrate, we opened another bottle of champagne, cut the cake and drank a lot of toasts. Then Greg suggested we should all go and dine with him. Naturally there was no opposition to that plan.

Our civil wedding was to be followed by a blessing the following day, Anzac Day, which commemorates the gallantry of Australian and New Zealand forces at Gallipoli in 1915. Reggie had served with the Indian Brigade at Gallipoli and had been invited to attend the Memorial Service at Westminster Abbey and I accompanied him. After the service we were told to wait until the rest of the congregation had left, and then we were shown into the King Henry VII chapel. Shortly after, the Dean came in and asked for God's blessing upon our marriage. The ceremony was all over in about ten minutes, and then the Dean left the altar and came to speak to us, and wished us the best of luck - it was a very moving and satisfying occasion. We then drove to the Hyde Park Hotel and had lunch, just the two of us. I don't remember what we ate, but Reggie ordered a very fine bottle of Burgundy, and we drank toasts to almost everyone in our extended families.

*General Sir Reginald Savory 1969*

# CHAPTER 15

## MARRIED LIFE AS LADY SAVORY  1969-1994

Reggie, through the family connections of his first wife, arranged for us to rent a cottage in the village of Seale, just off the Hog's Back near Farnham in Surrey. It was with much sorrow that I gave up my flat in West Kensington Court. I had been one of the first tenants to move there in 1937 and had probably spent the greater part of my life in that building, including most of the war years, and I felt very attached to it. However, I looked forward now to my new life with Reggie, and to the pleasures of living once again in the English countryside.

We spent nearly three years in the first cottage before moving next door into the Old Forge, renamed School Hill Cottage, which had been modernized for us. I had enjoyed the unaccustomed pleasure of planning the rooms of the cottage, especially the layout of the kitchen and sitting room, and for practical reasons I had insisted on a downstairs shower. Together, Reggie and I planned the garden, and the result gave us great joy. As we settled into our permanent home, I found myself entertaining many of his military colleagues, and dignitaries from the days of the Indian Raj. I particularly remember one Sunday, when Reggie returned from Seale Church and announced that a delegation from the Sikh regiment he had once commanded were in Seale and would be coming for lunch! Of course I was horrified at the prospect of feeding a regiment, but a few minutes later about twenty Sikhs, complete with colourful turbans, came in procession up School Hill bearing plates of steaming curries and other delicacies. Luckily it was a sunny day, so we were able to help ourselves and eat in the garden.

Reggie had become a military historian of some note with his book on the history of the British Army's campaign in Germany during the Seven Years War, and he regularly travelled to London to do the research for other writing projects, while I began to put some notes together for my own memoir. Nicky was divorced in 1971, and visited us from time to time, sometimes by himself, but often with one or more of my grandchildren, which was a great treat for me. Despite the discomforts of old age, I felt happy and settled for the first time in my life.

## The Georgian Girl

After over ten years of contented married life, Reggie suddenly developed a serious chest infection and was rushed to the military hospital in Aldershot. He was eighty-six years old and a few days later he died. It was 1980, and although the doctors would not admit it, I believed that he had contracted Legionnaires' Disease which was just developing at the time. Nicky flew over for the funeral and to give me comfort and support, but had to return almost immediately to his work in California.

In November 1980 I learned that Alan had died. I had loved him all my life and I believe he had loved me, but the tumult of events throughout the twentieth century had kept us apart. I did not attend his funeral but I mourned him deeply.

About a year later Nicky rang to say he was considering returning to England; could I put him up for a few months, until he found his feet? Of course I was delighted to do so, and he arrived with all his worldly belongings just in time for Christmas 1981. He moved into his own flat in London a few months later.

In 1987 there seemed to be a glimmer of hope for Russia. Mikhail Gorbachev was elected First Secretary of the Communist Party and, although determined to maintain communism in Russia, Glasnost (Openness) was bringing an important breakthrough in relations with the west. Mrs Thatcher, after meeting him, famously declared he was a man with whom she could do business. In October of that year Nicky went on a tour of Russia and Georgia and visited some of the places where I had grown up. He visited St Petersburg, still called Leningrad, Tiflis, where I was born while my father was building the oil pipeline from Baku to Batuum on the Black Sea, and Moscow, which I remember was of no great importance during pre-revolutionary Russia except as the seat of the Russian Orthodox Church. I was nervous about his visit and begged him not to reveal his Russian ancestry. I don't know whether he kept that promise, but he returned safely and with wonderful photographs of some places that I recognized, such as the Opera House in Tiflis, and the building in which we once had a flat. I was thrilled to see them and to learn that many Russians spoke to him in English, and that they all wanted better relations with the west. In November 1988 Nicky married Charlotte, and a year later Anne was born just as the Berlin Wall fell, bringing the Cold War to an end and freedom to the people of Eastern Europe.

I look back now at the events all those years ago, when I was seventeen and had expected to die, and I remember how incensed I was that my life would be taken at such a young age. But my life has been exciting and fulfilled and in my nineties I can look forward to a release from pain and from the endless tiredness that comes with old age. I feel that I have had a very good innings.

# The Georgian Girl

*Lady Savory was taken to hospital in her ninety-fourth year with heart and kidney failure and, although she recovered enough to return to School Hill Cottage, she died a few weeks later at her writing desk, on the evening of 22$^{nd}$ July, 1994.*

*Sir Reginald Savory at work at School Hill Cottage*

# The Georgian Girl

*Sir Reginald & Lady Savory off to a reception.*

# APPENDIX 1

The following extract is taken from Sir Reginald Savory's account of his time in Vladivostock 1919-1920, and is reprinted here with the kind permission of the Society for Army Historical Research.

> When World War I ended in November 1918, Captain Reginald Savory MC had been serving with the 14$^{th}$ Sikhs. At that time there was a call for volunteers to go to Siberia to join the British Military Mission there under General Knox and he at once offered to go. A few days later, he was informed that he had been selected for duty as an infantry and pioneer instructor with the Mission and was to proceed to Vladivostok as soon as possible.
> 
> On the afternoon of 16 April 1919, we sailed into Vladivostok harbour. At its entrance lay Russki Ostrov (Russian Island). We skirted its eastern end and entered the main harbour, known as Zolotoi Rog (Golden Horn). It was long, rather narrow and, as its name implies, horn shaped. It was far larger than we had anticipated. The commercial docks were at the entrance to the harbour, the naval dockyard further in, towards the tip of the horn. Two or three British ships were unloading at the commercial quays. In the naval enclave were a British cruiser (HMS Kent), an American cruiser and some Russian destroyers.
> 
> The town of Vladivostok was built along the northern and western slopes of the Golden Horn. On the hills behind the town were the stone forts of the harbour defences. Across the water, on the eastern side of the harbour, the country was rural and wooded. A few shacks, or "dachas", could be seen, and a little cultivation.
> 
> As the Monteagle steamed slowly in, we could see more of the town itself. There were railway yards and sidings, stretching the whole length of the waterfront. There was the main railway station, an imposing grey stone building, facing a square, with the usual collection of cabs and "droshkies". Across the square was another large building of barrack type, with Russian and British flags flying over it. It was a headquarters and I

## The Georgian Girl

*got to know it very well.*

*There appeared to be two streets. One ran past the railway station, and up over the high ground at the back of the town, where it seemed to peter out among wooden shacks and hovels. The other, the Svietlanskaya Ulitsa, ran roughly at right angles to it. Both these streets had side streets, running a short distance before stopping dead and leading nowhere. The two main streets were cobbled, the others were unmetalled, pot-holed, and bordered by the shacks and yards of the poor. In short, Vladivostok consisted of only two main thoroughfares and the waterfront, with their shops warehouses and quays.*

*After docking, we were led into a meeting room and put into the picture. There was an Anglo-Russian naval flotilla, operating on the River Kama, a tributary of the Volga. Its base was at Perm west of the Urals. This was a surprise. Here was the Royal Navy, right in the middle of the greatest landmass in the world, and apparently operating ahead of the army. By then our maps were out and we began to realize the vast area over which the operations were taking place.*

*There was to be an Anglo-Russian regiment, of all arms. It was to be composed of Russian troops, and to be trained by British officers and non-commissioned officers. Its station was to be in Omsk. It was to have a training centre for officer-cadets at Russian Island, Liaison officers were required, some with Russian fighting formations, others with the Russian staff, and a few with such characters as Ataman Semenov, the Cossack leader, who had established himself along the railway, where it ran through Manchuria.*

*I had been appointed staff-captain to the base headquarters of the mission at Vladivostok. My colleague was Captain Riviere of the Loyal North Lancashire Regiment. Our immediate boss was Colonel C.J. Wickham. From him we learned that the original intention of forming an allied fighting front along the Urals against the Germans had been overtaken by events. The armistice with the Germans had been signed. Our objective now was nothing less than the support of the White Russian forces against the Bolsheviks. The strategy was to push on west of the Urals to the railway at Kotlas and Viatka, thence to link up with the anti-Bolshevik forces from Archangel, and in conjunction with the White Army in South Russia, under Denikin, to march into Russia proper and to extinguish the Revolution.*

## The Georgian Girl

*In addition to the White Russians, there were Americans and Japanese, both with sizeable forces; there were also missions from France, Italy and China; there were Serbians and Poles; also missions representing the newly created Baltic States of Estonia, Latvia & Lithuania; and of course the Czechs. All had different reasons for being in Siberia, but it was commonly assumed that they were there to help the White Russians defeat the Bolsheviks.*

*On 26 April, only ten days after arriving, I wrote home, "The news from the front is good, and the Bolsheviks seem to be retiring at a good pace. The powers that be take a very optimistic view of the show, and say that, if things go on as they are at present, we should be in Moscow before the year is up....."*

*As for us, we lived under the protection of our own flag. Not only were we safe enough, but we lived a social life of a diplomatic type, exchanging calls and giving receptions as if we were in the capital city of one of the world's most stable countries. This did not go unnoticed. It was undoubtedly one of the contributory causes of the hatred for the "interventionists". We had won the war (World War I), peace had been signed, a weight had been lifted from our minds. No wonder we were light-hearted, we were also patronising. Even the White Russians resented us.*

*We were still full of enthusiasm, but the news from the front was rather discouraging. The Bolsheviks had started to advance. The fighting was not intense. The White Army was merely fed up, demoralised and retreating without putting up any resistance worth the name. It was the start of a withdrawal, which was not to stop until it had reached Vladivostok. Orders now came from England for our two battalions to go home, and for the mission to be gradually wound-up.*

*On the morning of 17 November 1919, the shooting began. We were now in the front line. The spread of Bolshevism was advancing much faster than the Red Army, so that when it did arrive, it was welcomed by the population. The railways were packed with refugee-trains going east, almost head to tail. Vladivostok's marshalling-yards had scarcely any parking space and were full of trains, packed with refugees, all struggling for survival.*

*We had many good friends among the Russian refugees. They had all come to Vladivostok from Russia proper at a time when it had seemed as if Siberia was to be built up into an anti-communist state under the rule of Admiral Kolchak. They had left their homes, taken with them such*

## The Georgian Girl

*jewels and other valuables as they possessed, bought tickets for the trans-Siberian express, or paid bribes for seats, and fled eastwards. Now they had literally reached the end of the line and most had reached the bottom of their purses.*

*We all had our special friends among them. There were General and Madame Zouraboff and their two daughters. Also General and Madame Inostrantsev and their daughter Mary, who was just a school girl.*

*December was a depressing month. The news from the front went from bad to worse. As December wore on the last of the American warships left. More British officers arrived from the front on their way home. General Knox too came down the line. He had been ordered home. His last task was to attend the Christmas party in the Sergeants' Mess on Christmas Eve. The next day, Boxing Day, he sailed.*

# APPENDIX 2

Curriculum Vitae of Nicholas Zouraboff, translated from a carbon copy originally in French.

*An engineer of Roads and Communications, Privy Councillor of the Russian State, I took my degree at the Institute of Roads and Communications (Bridges and Highways) at St. Petersburg.*

*Since then I have been in the continuous employment of the Russian Government for a period of forty years, notably until 1914 in the Administative Section of the Transcaucasian Railway Network, where I have had experience of all areas of both management and construction of the aforementioned network.*

*During this time, I took part in the construction of the Tiflis-Baku line, 540 Km; Tiflis-Kars, 280Km; Alexandropol-Erivanne-Djoulfa, 322Km; and Kars-Karaourgane, 100Km, as well as the laying of the oil pipe-line from Baku to Batuum, 840Km.*

*The Transcaucasian Railway, since its foundation, has used fuel-oil in lieu of coal to drive its locomotives, and this has given me unrivalled experience in the purchase, storage and use of this fuel.*

*At the beginning of 1914, 10th March, I was promoted to Chief Director of the Siberian Transbaikal Railway Network, which stretches for a distance of 1,800Km, and at the same time, I was made Chief Engineer for the project of building the second line of the railway round Lake Baikal, as well as being made the Administrator of the Ferry Boats and Flotilla of Lake Baikal, with a residence in Irkoutsk.*

*In June 1916, I was named President of the Far-Eastern Section (resident in Vladivostock) for Rail and River Transport, including the rail-networks of Transbaikal and the Sino-East, and the river-networks of the Amour and the Oussoury rivers, (covering altogether 6,000Km) together with all navigation on the river Amour.*

## The Georgian Girl

# APPENDIX 3

Translation of two letters written in Russian by General Nicholas S. Zouraboff to his daughter Marie Zouraboff. He addresses her as Blossie and she was often called Blossom by the family.

*Paris 9 December 1924*
*15-bis Boulevard Victor*

*My dear and kind Blossie,*

*Tomorrow, 10 December is your Birthday, the day that God gave me a baby girl. I will not forget the moment: it was two o'clock in the morning, I was lying in my office, dressed, on a mattress and was awaiting the results. Granny entered and informed me "tu as une petite gentille fille"; for some reason we all were expecting it would be a boy, then Granny left the office just as quietly as she came in with the news.*

*No boy could give me happiness, as much as you, my child. Tomorrow, as always, I am fully with you in spirit, love and hope. Live happily many, many decades with the happiness of all who love you; may the Lord God save you from all kinds of sorrows and sickness, of which I especially pray to God about your health, that you be strong physically as well as in spirit.*

*I hug and kiss you warmly, my wonderful friend, your loving Papa.*

# The Georgian Girl

*Boulogne sur Seine 28 June 1931*
*3-bis Avenue J.B. Clement*

*My dear Blossie*

*Forgive me that I have not answered your nice letter dated 9 June, but I have been very busy preparing for the Day of Culture on technical and economic subjects in Russia. And for this I waited until you returned to your flat, which you do not like and which you cannot leave.*

*Thank you to both of you for honouring me by naming the little boy with his third name "Nicholas". It is very far sighted and prudent to give the young person full freedom to choose his own name in the future, depending on social conditions and circumstances of life.*

*Thank God Mother has returned and feels very well; without her we have struggled for five months. With her arrival even Lily began to feel better from her ailment, which was very bad. She had stayed in bed the entire week, suffering severe head and ear aches. We did not know what to feed her and this resulted in weakness and loss of weight. Now, thank God she is better, but not entirely well.*

*I hope that the little one and you with Ian are in good health. We love you and wish you all good health.*

*Our Greggy has grown yet more and is busy with examinations to enter the next grade in school, where he is advancing well and behaves himself well. Often he asks me whom I prefer, him or the second grandson.*

*Kisses and hugs to all three of you.*

*Papa*

# APPENDIX 4

The day after their civil wedding at Caxton Hall, Sir Reginald and Lady Savory went to Westminster Abbey for a their marriage to be blessed after the Anzac Day Commemorative Service, and he describes the ceremony here, in an extract from a longer, unpublished account of the events of both days. Aileen Slim was the wife of Field-Marshall Lord Slim, who had been seriously wounded at Gallipoli.

> *The next day, 25<sup>th</sup> April, was also to be memorable for us. It was to be the occasion on which out marriage at Caxton Hall was to receive, so to speak, its religious seal. The 25<sup>th</sup> April is the day on which each year the gallantry of the Australian and New Zealand forces in the First World War is commemorated. It is chosen because that was the morning on which the Australians and New Zealanders first landed at Gallipoli in 1915. I myself was with the Indian Brigade in Gallipoli and at times served either with or alongside the Australians and New Zealanders. I am therefore an honorary Anzac. As such I attended the Anzac Memorial Service in Westminster Abbey together with my wife. We were shown to special seats in the very beautifully carved choir-stalls, which had been specially allotted to us for this occasion by the Dean of Westminster himself. We took up our seats a quarter of an hour or so before the service was due to start, and various people came in and occupied seats near and around us; the official representatives of the three Armed Services, the High Commissioners of Australia and New Zealand and also, I was very glad to note, a representative from the Indian Government. And just before the service started, in came no less a person than dear Aileen Slim. She was accompanied by other ladies, all of them either the wives of High Commissioners, or wives or widows of ex-Governors or Governors-General of Australia. Aileen recognized me at once and we had a short talk. I told her we were going after the service to Henry's VII's Chapel to receive the blessing there. I said we would be alone, just Maria and myself, but asked her to come along and make a quorum, and she said she would be delighted. So the Anzac Memorial Service took place, the choir came in,*

*the Dean was there in full robes, the singing of the anthem was beautiful, and the sermon was preached by one of the bishops of Australia. When the service was over, the Dean went to the altar and gave the blessing, and the congregation filed out.*

*Maria and I had been told by one of the Cathedral officials not to leave with the others but to wait until the rest had gone, and that then we would be shown into Henry VII's chapel. Gradually the Cathedral emptied. Then one of the officials came and asked us to follow him. Maria and I led the way followed by Aileen. We went through the iron gates leading in to Henry VII's chapel. There we waited. There were only four of us, Maria and myself, Aileen and a Naval Commander, whose name I forget, the official who was looking after us. After a while, in came a black-robed gentleman, preceding the Dean who was wearing full canonicals and looking extremely dignified. The Dean greeted us both, asked us to stand side-by-side in front of the Altar, then stood on the steps of the altar and said some appropriate prayers over us, and asked for God's blessing on our marriage. The short ceremony was all over in about ten minutes. Then the Dean left the altar, came and spoke to us, wished us the best of luck, and preceded by his black-robed usher left the chapel. Aileen was charming. She gave Maria such a sweet kiss; and gave me one too for which I was duly thankful. Then, having refused an invitation to lunch as she was already late for another she should have attended, she hurried away. Maria and I were then led by the Naval Commander who had been our usher during the proceedings, out of Henry VII's chapel. We walked sedately through crowds of waiting sightseers who had been kept out whilst our little Service was going on, down the aisle to the main gate where our car called for us and off we went. Altogether it had been for me, and I am sure for Maria too, a very moving and satisfactory dénouement (if one can use such a word) to our marriage.*

*We then drove smartly to the Hyde Park Hotel and had lunch, just the two of us. I don't know what we ate but I do know that we had a bottle of the most excellent Burgundy. We drank toasts to almost everybody – to Nick and June; to Lily and Greg; to one or two of my relations; and to all sorts of other people. That bottle of Burgundy did not last nearly as long as I had thought it would, and I confess it was I who drank the greater share of it.*

ISBN 142512935-8